Men and the Language of Emotions

Also by Dariusz Galasiński

CULTURAL STUDIES AND DISCOURSE ANALYSIS *(with Chris Barker)*

THE LANGUAGE OF DECEPTION

THE LANGUAGE OF BELONGING *(with Ulrike Hanna Meinhof)*

Men and the Language of Emotions

Dariusz Galasiński

Professor of Discourse and Cultural Studies
University of Wolverhampton
United Kingdom

First published 2004 by
PALGRAVE MACMILLAN
Houndmills, Basingstoke, Hampshire RG21 6XS and
175 Fifth Avenue, New York, N.Y. 10010
Companies and representatives throughout the world

PALGRAVE MACMILLAN is the global academic imprint of the Palgrave
Macmillan division of St. Martin's Press, LLC and of Palgrave Macmillan Ltd.
Macmillan® is a registered trademark in the United States, United Kingdom
and other countries. Palgrave is a registered trademark in the European
Union and other countries.

ISBN 0–333–99574–0

This book is printed on paper suitable for recycling and made from fully
managed and sustained forest sources.

A catalogue record for this book is available from the British Library.

Library of Congress Cataloging-in-Publication Data
Galasiński, Dariusz.
    Men and the language of emotions / Dariusz Galasiński.
        p. cm.
    Includes bibliographical references and index.
    ISBN 978-0-230-55431-3
    1. Men—Psychology. 2. Men—Identity.
    3. Emotions. 4. Masculinity. 5. Men—Language.
    I. Title.
    HQ1090.G33 2004
    155.3′32—dc22   2004051507

10   9   8   7   6   5   4   3   2   1
13 12 11 10 09 08 07 06 05 04

Transferred to digital printing 2008

Rodzicom

Contents

Acknowledgements

This book owes its existence to a number of people who helped or supported me when I was designing and writing it. To give justice and thank all of them would be impossible. I would like, however, to acknowledge my indebtedness to Chris Barker, without whom the idea of this book would never have formed. Sally Johnson's comments and critique made the book much more presentable. Discussions with my colleagues and especially my graduate students in the University of Opole, where I held a visiting chair, and particularly with Marzena Ryba and Olga Kozłowska, provided me with a most fruitful venue to discuss and try out new ideas. Needless to say, all the book's shortcomings are my own.

My thanks also go to Jill Lake, my editor at Palgrave Macmillan, for starting our conversation in Reading and believing in the book.

Finally, I would like to thank Ola, Michał, and Ania for bearing with me and making this book a temporary member of our family.

DARIUSZ GALASIŃSKI

Transcription Conventions

[	beginning of overlapping speech
=	latching (no gap or no overlap between stretches of talk)
.	falling intonation
?	rising intonation
-	self-interruption
(.)	short pause
(..)	longer pause
wo:rd	lengthening
WORD	emphasis
(word)	word unclear
((word))	transcriber's comment.

1
Men and their Emotions

...where no one has felt before

'Your desire to explore space is inefficient, your need for familial connections is a weakness.' This is how Seven of Nine, one of *Star Trek: Voyager*'s main characters, a former human assimilated by the Borg (some dangerous and violent aliens), described humanity. It is a species driven by emotions. Indeed, one of *Star Trek*'s *topoi* is the juxtaposition of the emotional humans with the unemotional non-humans. First, there was Mr Spock, the cool and rational Vulcan, the butt of the volatile Captain Kirk's jokes in the original series. Then, in *The Next Generation*, came Lieutenant Commander Data, an android in pursuit of humanity, a quest for (amongst others) the chance to feel human emotions, understand jokes, and to love Lal, his android 'daughter'. Seven of Nine, a Borg, on the other hand, had to be pushed into humanity, especially since it implied giving up her orderly rationality and espousing the uncontrollability of emotions. Finally, another Vulcan, Subcommander T'Pol in the latest series, *Enterprise*, is also constructed as providing the cool and rational alternative to her captain's more cavalier attitude.

One of the significant traits of what it means to be human is to be able to feel emotions. It is so human that in one of the feature films based on the television series (*Generations*), the Data character, who had by then been equipped with an 'emotion chip', cannot handle himself in a dangerous situation; the emotion is much too much for him to control. Bewildered by the experience, Data is even more in admiration of his human ideals, those who are able to feel emotions and not be overwhelmed by them.

The moment we leave the friendly and not so friendly aliens, or the more or less likely future, and come back from where no one had gone before, however, we find that the issue of human emotionality is not so simple and straightforward as we might have imagined watching *Star Trek*. This is because, as much as the human race comprises men and women, it is only one of the two groups that is assumed either to have the ability to feel emotions, or to be able or want to express them in some way. The cultural models of men and masculinity are more often than not associated with the lack of emotionality. Apparently, a man is tough, does not share his pain, does not grieve and avoids warm feelings (see Jansz, 2000).

This book is about how men talk about their emotions. I want to demonstrate that men not only talk about their emotional experiences, but also relate them to men in general and masculinity. In this sense, this book is polemical. I intend to challenge not only these prevalent cultural models and stereotypes but, more importantly, quite a lot of academic constructs which describe masculinity as in one way or another emotionally impotent.

I shall develop two lines of argument throughout the book. First, I am interested in the relationship of emotions and emotionality with such constructs as masculinity, men, and gender identity. In contrast to quite a lot of academic writing on masculinity (see below), I am not really interested in constructing yet another model of masculinity, a theoretical construct whose rationale would basically be grounded in my own perception of reality, and underpinned by similar theoretical constructs. This book is data-driven because I am interested in real stories told by real men, with their own relevancies and constructions. Speaking about men, masculinity and masculine identities (and I shall problematise these concepts), I am predominantly concerned with their 'lived' versions. I would like to find out how men themselves construct their emotions in different contexts in relation to their identities. Second, I am also interested in the strategies men employ when they talk about their emotions. I shall explore these strategies, however, not only as some more or less abstract ways of speaking, but in terms of how they fulfil social functions. The way people speak about their emotions, as Bamberg (1997a, b) observed, is tied to the local context of interaction in which what is said furthers speakers' communicative goals.

It is important to note that in contrast to most linguistic research on emotions in language, I am not interested in how people express emotion in discourse (Ochs and Schieffelin, 1989; de Beaugrande, 1992; Caffi and Janney, 1994; Bloch, 1996; see also Gallois, 1993; Planalp, 1999). There are relatively few studies of discourse strategies employed by people accounting for, explaining, or simply telling stories about their emotions (see, e.g., Shimanoff, 1985; Lutz, 1990, 1996; Kidron and Kuzar, 2002). My study attempts to redress this paucity.

Before the arguments can be made, however, I need to clarify my 'starting points', the assumptions I shall be making with reference to three major research issues. Thus in what follows, I shall first review some literature on emotions, and second, I shall position my considerations in relation to debates on gender and masculinity. Third, I shall also discuss literature on masculinity and emotionality. These reviews are not really designed as comprehensive literature reviews; that would be beyond the scope of this book. Rather, they are aimed at indicating the theoretical stance I take in contrast to some (and in line with other) research. Finally, in the remainder of the chapter, I shall briefly indicate my approach to the analytical methods which I shall use in the analytic chapters.

Emotions

In *Psychology of Emotion*, Strongman (1996) makes a reference to 150 theories of emotion. There are countless more texts, articles and pieces of research. Even though researched widely, emotions are still somewhat elusive as regards their final definition (Oatley and Jenkins, 1996; see also Kemper, 1991; Shields, 1991). This research is so vast and varied that even a brief overview thereof is considerably beyond the scope of this chapter and book.

In his overview of research on emotion, Williams (2001) proposes that the main axis of debate in research on emotions is that of biology versus society. To what extent are emotions biological in origin, universal to humanity, physiological in their nature, and independent of both context and culture? Alternatively, to what extent are they particular to cultures and societies, learnt through socialisation and language (discourse) acquisition, context-dependent (see also Besnier, 1995)? My approach to emotions falls very strongly into the latter category. In contrast to scholars representing the quantitative approach to emotions, assuming their universalism (see contributions to Ekman and Davidson, 1994, or to Clark, 1992), I think of emotions as culture- and context-bound. There are two strands of emotion research I would like to mention here and claim affinity to: first, the cognitive linguistic research focused around that of Anna Wierzbicka (1999; see also 1988, 1995, 1998) and her quest to find 'semantic primitives' (a lexicon of basic concepts with which to define the lexicon); and second, the constructionist account of emotions.

Wierzbicka and those who follow this line of research (see, e.g., Goddard, 2002; Pavlenko, 2002b; contributions to Athanasiadou and Tabakowska, 1998; see also Kövecses, 1988, 1990, 1991) postulate an inherent link between emotions and the linguistic resources which are at people's disposal to label them. They oppose the view that people feel some universal emotions, as Lazarus (1991, 1995) would have it, that they all feel the same emotions (such as anger or sadness), regardless of what they may call them. We could only pose the question: how can we actually know that they all feel the same, if the only way they can actually tell us about it is through the medium of natural language?

The line of research assuming universality of emotions can perhaps be usefully shown at work when one views its cross-cultural application, in which questionnaires are used in different cultures and languages but apparently with reference to the same emotions. Thus Fischer and Manstead (2000) use the ISEAR (International Survey on Emotion Antecedents and Reactions) questionnaire in a study of gender emotional differences. The questionnaire, applied in 37 countries, covers experiences of seven emotions: joy, fear, anger, sadness, disgust, shame and guilt. The countries in which the questionnaire was applied included Poland and, as a native speaker of Polish, I cannot help wondering how it was done. There are two words for 'anger' in Polish (*złość* and *gniew*), neither an equivalent of *anger* (see also Wierzbicka 1999); there are at least two equivalents of *fear* (Polish *strach* and *lęk*, although the Polish word *obawa* is semantically not far away from the two). There is no equivalent of English *disgust*, and the equivalent of *guilt* (Polish *wina*) is a word from a legal-moral vocabulary and cannot be used to refer to emotional states. It is quite hard to see how the questionnaire could possibly be implemented in Poland without significant adaptation, which then, of course, defeats the point of comparability.

In such studies English is taken as a sort of super-language whose structures are not only transparent but, even more importantly, are universal across languages and cultures (an assumption which can be quite easily shown to be erroneous). Moreover, it is precisely the assumption of English as the predominant medium of research that leads scholars to theories of 'basic emotions', as assumptions are made also about sadness, fear, anger, disgust, shame and enjoyment (Ekman, 1992, 1993). Had Ekman done his research in Polish, quite apart from the problems with 'disgust', he would not have put 'enjoyment' on his list of basic emotions. There is no such word in Polish (for further critique see also Enfield and Wierzbicka, 2002).

Strong as this critique is and as much as the cognitive linguistic approach to emotions shows the cultural embeddedness of emotions, it has a significant shortcoming. Proposing to analyse emotions as semantic categories, it does not take full account of the fact that people can and in fact do use emotion words in different ways and in different contexts. Cognitive linguistics does not take full account of the context of the interaction in which people get emotional. This is a shortcoming which is catered for by the constructionist approach to emotions (see, e.g., Harré, 1986b; Harré and Stearns, 1995; Harré and Parrot, 1996; Lupton, 1998). The constructionist approach to emotions shares the concern of cognitive linguistics that emotions vary across cultures. Such studies as Lutz's (1988) account of Ifaluk discourse of emotions and the inapplicability of Western emotional categories are a good case in point (see also Stearns, 1995; and contributions to Lutz and Abu-Lughod, 1990). Emotions are historical (Zeldin, 1998) and tied to the context in which they are evoked (Bamberg, 1997a, b; see also Shields and MacDowell, 1987). Indeed there is evidence from research into bilingualism suggesting that 'in the process of second language socialization some adults may transform their verbal repertoires and conceptualizations of emotions, or at least internalize new emotion concepts of scripts' (Pavlenko, 2002a:71; see also Wierzbicka, 1994). But constructionism goes further in that it positions emotions as contextually embedded social practice.

Criticising psychology for making an ontological claim of the existence of emotions based upon physiological states sometimes associated with them, Harré (1986a) proposes that emotions are about interpreting, ordering and selecting ways in which to put the 'emotional experience' in language. This is done, in turn, only insofar as the linguistic resources and social practices allow us to. Constructionists view emotions as being inextricably linked to language, or (more accurately) the discursive practices associated with them. As Harré (1991) put it succinctly, to be angry is to take the angry position. Even love, sometimes wild and all-consuming, is constructed through confessions of love (necessarily labelling it, telling it, making stories about it), combined with socially accepted ways of talking about love (Wetherell, 1996). Emotions, in other words, do not happen to us: we bring them into existence through our discursive practices (Hearn, 1993). Bamberg (1997a, b) takes the link between discourse and emotions even further. Arguing for a more context-bound account of emotions, he posits that reporting one's emotions (caused by others), or someone else's (caused by the reporter), is done for different discursive purposes: one attributes blame, the other saves face. They must be seen, therefore, to pertain to different discursive practices, rather than to the all-encompassing category of 'emotion' or 'emotion talk' (see also Rosenberg, 1990).

To sum up, I shall see emotions as discursive practices, as ways of speaking, rather than as some internal states associated with physiological conditions of our bodies (incidentally, Ginsburg and Harrington, 1996, point out that there is little evidence that emotions can be reliably differentiated by physiological patterns). They may be, however, ways of accounting for bodily sensations which are learnt and subject to sanction by social practice, yet they are not names for such sensations (Harré, 1986a).

Adopting such a theoretical approach to emotions has a significant consequence for the kind of analyses I shall be attempting throughout the book. At one level, they will provide insight into certain discursive patterns as well as lived models of gender and emotionality. But patterns of men's speaking about emotions will also give insight into masculine emotionality (should there be any such thing) and the cultural rules governing it. As Harré and Stearns (1995:4) propose, there are vocabularies which 'track, correct, comment upon and manage our emotional feelings and displays. These are as much part of the total complex that adds up to the "psychology" of emotion as the expressions and feelings, and more so than the reactions of the limbic system!'

Gender and masculinity

Bourdieu (2001), in his account of masculine domination, states that the division between men and women appears to be 'in the order of things'; it is perceived to be so normal that it becomes inevitable. This is the 'lived' version of gender. People perceive gender as part of the core identity, the deepest selfhood, rather than not suspecting that it in fact might be a discursive product (van Langenhove and Harré, 1993). And it is as a discursive accomplishment that I shall see gender and gender identity. I shall take the anti-essentialist view of gender, thinking of it not so much as a fixed state but, rather, a process of becoming. Gender is a verb, as was aptly put by Johnson (1997). People construct themselves as male and female, as masculine and feminine, and Edley and Wetherell (1995) go so far as to suggest also that biological sex might be a cultural construct.

Let us start from the beginning. Connell (2002; see also 2000) proposes that gender is a social structure that centres upon our bodies, and particularly the reproductive area. It is a way in which society handles the human body. It means, continues Connell, that gender might not only differ sharply from one culture to another (see also Gilmore, 1990), but also that gender arrangements are linked to power relations, on the one hand reproducing and maintaining gender relations and, on the other hand, constraining social and gendered actors in their individual actions. It also means that gender is dynamic, historical, subject to change. There are, finally, four aspects of gender: power relations, production relations, emotional relations and symbolic relations.

It is within such a social structure that people construct themselves as men or women, and thus construct their gender identity. We could start with Butler (1990) and her theory of performance. Starting from the act of gender endowment – 'It's a girl' – a human subject is put into a regulatory frame within which she performs femininity, or it is performed for her, especially at the beginning of her life (McIlvenny, 2002b). Gender is achieved in situated conduct (West and Zimmerman, 1987; see also Cameron, 1997; McIlvenny, 2002a). Changing perspective, Morgan (1992) proposes that masculinity is something that is done (see also Whitehead, 2002). Beynon (2002) sees it in terms of sets of signs, and Brittan (1989) adds that masculinities are always local and subject to change (for a review of definitions of masculinity, see Connell, 1995; also Clatterbaugh, 1997).

Scholars propose at the same time, however, that masculinity or masculinities are configurations of practice (Connell, 2000) within gender relations. Morgan (1992), despite his pronouncements of masculinities being performed in context, also proposes that masculinities are sets of practices which reproduce a gender system. Whitehead and Barrett (2001) speak of behaviours, languages and practices (see also Walker, 1994; Pujolar, 2000; Barrett, 2001). We are dealing with at least a dual understanding of masculinity (and femininity, for that matter). On the one hand, masculinity is an accomplishment in the local situation, a gender identity, always provisional, always subject to change (see, e.g., Barker and Galasiński, 2001; Kerfoot, 2001). Alternatively, masculinity is seen as a system of practices, or perhaps systems of practices; it is a more abstract construct whether lived or academic. Indeed, Beynon provides what seems to be a useful list of the social factors impacting masculinity. He lists: historical location, age and physique, sexual orientation, education, status and lifestyle, geography, ethnicity, religion and beliefs, class and occupation, culture and subculture (Beynon, 2002:10). There are as many masculinities – presumably in the sense of configurations of practice – as there are configurations of such social factors (see also a critique of the notion of masculinity in Hearn, 1996).

Understanding masculinity as a locally negotiated identity is relatively straightforward, as it ties in with the anti-essentialist understanding of identity. In such understanding identity is a discursive construct: there is no fixed inner essence of self. Identity is a discourse of (not) belonging, similarity and difference, which is continually negotiated and renegotiated within a localised social context. Identity is therefore a continual process of becoming: it is always provisional, always subject to change. But the problem of masculinity as a configuration of practices is considerably more difficult. What exactly is meant by it? Is it about the identifiable practices of biological men? Indeed, Morgan (1992) proposes that seeing a group of men, one can always infer masculinity: not as an inherent trait, but as practice. Men are always masculine in this understanding of masculinity. But such a stance is quite problematic since it seems to assume that one can infer masculinity just on the basis of looking at biological men. Given the plurality of masculinities, which masculinity would that be? Could it not be possible for such biological men to be feminine (Kerfoot, 2001)?

However, one can incorporate the notion of configuration of practice into the concept of masculinity. Ochs (1992), for example, proposes that masculinity is a pattern of behaviour that becomes associated with being male (see also Tannen, 1999; Edley, 2001). It is a societal construction of masculinity, a social construct more akin to a stereotype, which thus reduces masculinity to biology or some non-negotiable identity core, except that it is mediated by the perceptions of biologically underpinned 'sex categories' (West and Zimmerman, 1987). Such social constructions and representations of masculinity are, in other words, ideologies of men and masculinity (on ideology see van Dijk, 1998). This is an understanding of masculinity seconded by Bordo (1997), who proposes that masculinity is related to ideologies and representations of gender, idealisations which can be aspired to as much by men as by women. What is important to remember is that masculinity in this understanding has little to do with the locally constructed masculine identities, even though it might, of course, act as the regulatory frame in which social actors construct themselves. Such ideologies are constructed both by individual and public discourses, with various social and communicative purposes, with various audiences. They are unlikely to be homogeneous and without contradictions. Indeed, evidence from public representations of masculinity suggests that they are anything but (e.g., Chapman, 1988; Rutherford, 1988; Edwards, 1997). In this sense, of course, one can speak of a number (likely to be finite, I think) of masculinities. The construct of masculinity I have arrived at consists of two elements: the locally constructed masculine identity, and masculinity in the sense of gender ideology, with nothing in between, no notion of masculinity as a set of practices performed by men, whether understood in terms of sex or gender.

In her discussion of gender negotiation in the local context, Cameron (1997) points out not only that men and women do not mechanically reproduce the 'appropriate' gender behaviours they have learnt in the process of socialisation, but they also learn a broader set of gendered meanings which enter into complex relationships with the way people speak. In a quite radically contextual account of masculinities, Johnson (1997) not only rejects what she calls the 'all-purpose male oppressor', but also points out that the unfixedness of gender identities makes it quite difficult to imagine the linguistic resources used in their construction. Johnson suggests that masculine identities – while tied to the local context of interaction – cannot be easily associated with linguistic or discursive patterns with which to construct them systematically. Johnson's point puts in doubt the issue of masculinity as a pattern of men's interactions. This point is made more forcefully by Hearn (1996; see also McMahon, 1993) who rejects the notion of pre-conceived existence of masculinity as reification of the social construction. MacInnes (1998) goes even further, proclaiming the 'end of masculinity' and proposing that masculinity is no more than ideology.

Indeed, I would add that the list of social factors listed by Beynon (2002), apart from the obvious lack of the able-bodied and disabled axis (which can clearly impact both representations of masculinity as well as masculine identities), does not involve personal experience, regardless of those demographics. Surely, my performance of masculine identities will be affected by what kind of parents I had, what kind of values they passed on to me and to what extent they became mine. Is the fact that I accidentally knocked out two of a friend's teeth during a football match relevant? I can still feel the mark of his teeth on my forehead; he still misses his two front teeth; and I have not played football ever since. Illness, trauma, accidents, political systems, military systems, and imprisonment will all have some impact upon individual men's life-stories, and thus, I would argue, potentially, upon their gender identity constructions, at least in certain contexts. Trying to capture all that diversity under a category of a configuration of practice seems to me quite unrealistic.

In what sense do men 'do masculinity' then? Well, only in the sense of constructing themselves as men in the local context of interaction. The configurations of practice by which Connell or Morgan define masculinity are not much more than social constructs, and men do not construct them as part of their identity, even though there is probably little doubt that in constructing themselves as men, as I said before, men are constrained by such ideologies. But the rejection of masculinity as some sort of practice men perform as social actors has another consequence. It was put succinctly by Johnson who rejects the idea that men should be some linguistically homogeneous group of people. There is no reason, continues Johnson, 'why the discursive strategies used by *individual men* should be consistent – either from one situation, or even from one utterance to the next' (Johnson 1997:21; emphasis in the original).

This argument, with which I agree, puts in question quite a lot of research into the so-called female/feminine or male/masculine language. There is literature, some of it still very recent, which portrays men and women in terms of particular conversational styles, certain kinds of expressions, certain kinds of language (for a classical study see R. Lakoff, 1973). Most recently, Mulac, Bradac and Gibbons (2001) proposed that men's language could be defined as direct, succinct, instrumental, and women's in opposite terms (see also Tannen, 1998). Coates (1997b) talks about and men's avoidance of self-disclosure (see also Reid and Fine, 1992; Gough and Edwards, 1998). Holmes (1995) proposes that women use compliments more often than men and that these are of a different kind (for other analyes see also Coates, 1997, 1999; for a critique see Talbot, Atkinson and Atkinson, 2003). Ochs and Taylor (1995) ascribe dominant narrative modes to men/fathers; Adams, Towns and Gavey (1995) discuss rhetorical devices which men use in legitimising their violence against women. While offering interesting insights into context-situated talk, these studies offer hardly any evidence that they are in any way typical of men (or women), or that they have anything to do with masculinity (or femininity), or indeed, gender.

Goodwin (2002) provides a convincing critique of such studies. Analysing girls-only conversations she shows that domination is far from being part of only either cross-gender talk, or male conversations. Her insight into what she calls 'the darker side of female interactions of exclusion' (Goodwin, 2002:727; see also Baxter, 2002) is probably less to do with gender and more to do with the dynamic of power relations underpinning peer-group dynamics. As I said, I have no doubt that such studies are very useful insights into how people speak in certain situations, but I doubt very much that they offer any insight into gendered language. Thus, to borrow Cameron's (1998a) distinction, such studies demonstrate some facts about language used by men or women as an an empirical category, but give no insights into women's or men's language. Cameron points out further that the complexity of the relationship between the two categories should not be underestimated. I think that Cameron's view is probably rather too weak. If gender identity is unfixed, dynamic, a process of becoming (even if not haphazard and not without constraints), surely one cannot square it with a female or male language. Allowing for such a category would we not fix gender, tie it down to a linguistic structure or discursive strategy? To sum up, I view masculinity in two dimensions. On the one hand, it is to do with the locally negotiated identities, always provisional, always in a state of flux. It is men's performance of being a man, always done anew, always in a particular local context. I think women cannot perform masculinity in this sense, just as men cannot perform femininity. On the other hand, masculinity is a social construct, a gender ideology, a society's way of associating certain practices with gender. Here masculinity can be seen as a configuration of social practices, but these practices are not there to be read off what men say or do; they are mediated by the society's ideological constructs. In this sense, but not in the previous sense, it is also possible for women to be thought of as masculine and men as feminine (see also Bordo, 1997). Local performances of men and women can include such behaviours or actions which are normally associated with the other gender.

What I have rejected here is the intermediate level of masculinity as men's practices, not only because of the plurality of masculinities, but also, simply, the plurality of men who, while acting within social frameworks of gender ideologies, are also capable of negotiating these frameworks in a variety of way. Gender, as Lloyd (1999) proposes, is always a 'repetition with a difference'. The argument of masculinity at a level between the local context and ideology, in the form of social practice, would inevitably lead to an essentialisation of masculinity. Moreover, one could theoretically imagine an infinite number of such 'configurations of practice' associated with the various criss-crossings impacting upon what it means to be a man. I do not think we need such a construct to account for social life, the way men construct themselves through discourse, and the way society constructs them in doing so.

This is not to say that we, as analysts, will not be able to observe certain patterns in constructions of identities, but precisely because of the men's submergence in ideologies and society's narratives of what it means to be a man. In their local negotiation of identities, men of course make use of such discourses and practices which they associate with masculinity; this is indeed why we normally would expect men to be dressed in particular clothes, in a particular way. But my argument is that while people speak 'the way one speaks', that people dress 'the way one dresses', it does not mean that such practices are linked to masculinity in some sort of essential way.

Masculinity and emotions

Before I discuss the literature on the relationship between masculinity and emotionality, I would like to say a few words about Western models of emotions. I believe that it is also these models which are responsible for the host of assumptions about whether and how men experience and express their emotions. According to Lutz (1988; see also Parrott, 1995; Howard, Tuffin and Stephens, 2000), the Western view of emotions sees them as in opposition to rational thought (as in anger) as well as indicating withdrawal or disengagement (as in sadness). Moreover, emotions are seen as unintended and uncontrollable: they are dangerous and render people vulnerable. They are physical and natural, and thus in opposition to civilisation. Fischer and Jansz (1995) add animality as a cultural characteristic of emotions. Bodor (1997) posits, moreover, that the emotions and their displays are always open to criticism and that social actors, especially adults, must always be able to give a reasonable account of their emotional experience. This is seconded by Fischer and Jansz (1995) who analysed 'emotion narratives', which are accounts of emotions explaining emotional experiences, making them intelligible to other people. It is fair to say, I think, that today's Western outlook on emotions is more negative than positive. While we may like having emotions, we do not want to lose control over our actions or bodies. But if you want to stay in control, and men – at least stereotypically – are thought to want it more than anything, emotionality cannot be good for them. Men cannot be emotional; *men don't cry* is a saying that has versions in different languages across Europe.

What I shall argue below, however, is that such stereotypes are likely to be the basis of quite a few academic models of masculinity, especially those which are attempts at 'theorising' masculinity, with little or no (or even contradictory) empirical grounding. Indeed, the review of the literature on gender and emotionality leads to the view of significant contradictions in the field. One can almost think of any stance on gender and emotion, and find it in the literature (for a critique of psychological research into gender and emotions, see Fischer, 1993; see also Brody, 1985). Thus you can easily find texts which state happily that there is growing evidence on the gendered nature of emotions and the fact that men and women differ quite significantly in the ways they express these (verbally, behaviourally and non-verbally) and in physiological arousal (see, e.g., Shields, 1987, 1990, 1995; Brody, 1993, 1997, 2000; Fischer 1995; Kelly and Hutson-Comeaux, 1999; Fischer and Manstead, 2000; Fivush and Buckner, 2000; Jansz, 2000). But you can also find, although there are considerably fewer such texts, literature on gender and emotion in which such differences are significantly played down and it is similarities which are stressed (see, e.g., Shimanoff; 1985; J. T. Johnson and Shulman, 1988; Fischer and Jansz, 1995; Anderson and Leaper, 1998; Barrett *et al.*, 1998).

Despite the occasional claims to the contrary, the problem with this kind of research is that it almost invariably does not problematise gender in its research methodology, positioning men and women as two uniform groups of people. Gender is assumed to provide people with some sort of 'core identity' (Shields, 2002; see also Shields, 2000) which is hardly negotiable, or something that can in fact be measured (e.g., Thompson, Pleck and Ferrera, 1992; Pleck, Sonenstein and Ku, 1993). The frequent use of questionnaires supposedly referring to emotions, when in fact they are not much more than lexical labels, makes the research even more problematic (see, however, Shields and Crowley, 1996). But however much one may disagree with the theoretical stances and methodological procedures of social psychological research, still the conclusion of men's alleged lack of emotionality is drawn from the research data the scholars collect in their laboratories. What is quite puzzling is that there is quite a lot of scholarship which incorporates the claim of men's emotional incompetence at the level of assumption, as something that does not need to be argued; it is simply there.

Let me start with Seidler, probably the most severe critic of masculine emotionality. Seidler (1994:30) writes:

> we never learn to share our feelings with those we are close to, thinking of this as a form of 'self-indulgence' that might be expected of women but it is inexcusable for men, we never really learn to *share* ourselves. And it is true that as men we are constantly holding ourselves back even from those with whom we are most intimate.

Indeed, elsewhere Seidler (1989) reveals that he has been often challenged for not giving enough of himself in his relationships. Lupton (1998:114), finally, quotes Seidler saying: 'We do not know what we feel. We do not have the words to express what is happening to us, nor a sense of how emotional and personal lives have been disorganised' (see also Seidler, 1992).

Clare seconds these views in a more popular recent account of masculinity in which he never pauses to question his assumption of unemotional men. He writes (Clare, 2001:212): 'At the heart of the crisis in masculinity is a problem with the reconciliation of the private and the public, the intimate and the impersonal, the emotional and rational.' Men allegedly cannot muster, and are left to admire, the emotional frankness of women.

Middleton (1992) proposes that men have lost their language of emotions (see also Tolson, 1977), while Horrocks (1994) states that men are emotionally impotent and inarticulate. Coates (2003) proposes that the vast majority of men's narratives are characterised by emotional restraint, a trait found particularly in white middle-class and middle-aged men. Rutherford (1988) sees only the 'traditional' masculinity in the form of his 'retributive man' along these lines. Brittan (1989) speaks about men's commitment to rationality as a form of exclusion of other forms of experience. Duncombe and Marsden (1995, 1998; see also Kerfoot, 2001) not only see masculinity as emotionally distant, but propose that all the emotional labour in relationships is done by women (on male–female friendships, see also Swain, 1992). Finally, Giddens (1992) not only has little doubt as to the different emotional styles of men and women, but he also prefers that of women. Whitehead (2002) supports his earlier view that emotional intimacy remains forever in the distance, with men shunning it (see also Stearns, 1979).

Interestingly, Lupton (1998), in her study of 'the emotional self', while acknowledging masculine emotionality still makes the implicit assumption of the 'unemotional man'. Saying that 'men are making concerted efforts to express their emotions' (p. 132), Lupton positions men's emotionality as something of a Herculean labour in pursuit of expressing an emotion or two. Shields (2002) takes a different approach to the problem of masculine inexpressivity, suggesting that men's lack of emotionality seems to have more to do with their talking about their emotions.

However, to say that men do not feel or do not express emotions is almost intuitively implausible. Thus Lupton (1998) proposes that models of 'unemotional man' do not take note of the fact that men are 'frequently' angry, aggressive and jealous (emotions which frequently lead to violence). Indeed, such a view is seconded by Hearn (1993:143) who talks about men being 'too emotional, too out of control'. One immediately thinks about figures often quoted in the literature on men, which reveal that most of the violent crime in Western countries is committed by men (e.g., Connell, 1995). And yet it does not seem to me obvious that crimes perpetrated by violent men have to be underpinned by violent emotions (whatever these might actually be), or that this extremely regrettable state of affairs can be extrapolated to men and masculinity in general. Still, the model of the 'angry men' is only a partial alternative to that of the 'unemotional man' since it constructs masculinity in terms of 'negative' emotions; men are still impotent insofar as the 'positive' go.

The assumptions about the emotional incompetence of men are not only at the general level of theorising about men. Coates, in what I think is a first book-length study of men's language, takes the assumptions to her data and, while ignoring the form of the narrative, simply applies the model.

Thus, Coates (2003:49) quotes the following fragment of a narrative by a middle-aged man who tells a story about collapsing due to acute appendicitis (for ease, I omit some of Coates's transcription marks):

the next morning things were no better
so. I walked around the street a couple of hundred yards to the doctor's
    surgery
unfortunately. the doctor. lived out in Essex
and he'd been snowed in
so. I spent a couple of hours sitting around in his surgery
and then finally the receptionist says, 'Look you know,
the doctor isn't going to be able to make it till this evening,
he's stuck in the snow,
would you mind coming back'.
so I shuffled off around the street
and spent the day thinking you know 'This is really getting bad',
because .hhhh oddly enough the sort of classic appendicitis pain
    didn't appear until very late
you know 'god only knows what is wrong with me,
but this is – this is definitely rough'.
so I spent the whole day day um –
finally five or so. o'clock came round
and I staggered around the street to the doctor's surgery
and this time I got to see him
and I was going like this
sort of swaying in the breeze

and he said 'I need to get you a bed,
suspected appendicitis' he said.

Coates comments that the speaker shows incredible stoicism, that
this is a story of heroism. She writes further: 'The protagonist has to
endure a terrible ordeal; he becomes increasingly ill, and circumstances,
such as bad weather, conspire against him. He comes though the ordeal
with stoic fortitude' (Coates, 2003:50). I cannot see another explanation
of Coates's interpretation except for the 'unemotional man' stereotype/
model. It seems to me that the quoted narrative is a story of an ill man,
quite helpless in his illness, waiting in fear for his doctor to provide
help. It might also be a story of luck (cheating death, if you like). There
are three aspects of the story I would like to point out.

First, it is a story of waiting. Despite the fact that the speaker tells his
story in agentive terms, all his actions are the result of either the doctor
not coming in, or the receptionist telling him to go home. He is hardly
a man endowed with the power to decide about himself, being rather at
the mercy of the receptionist telling him what to do. So, the man goes
to see the doctor (just about the only thing he does of his own accord),
waits there without a murmur, and then is sent home to wait some
more.

It is also a story of weakness, not of toughing it out. Having been sent
home, meekly, he does not merely walk back, he shuffles back, his
physical weakness already obvious (once again, hardly indicative of
heroism: heroes do not shuffle, I think). But the weakness grows and
the speaker, perhaps dramatising his account to make it even more
tellable, even more one of 'being within a whisker', talks about staggering
back to the surgery, another action indicating weakness rather than
heroism. The story reaches its finale at the point when the speaker is
barely able to stand upright on his feet.

Third, and important, I think it is a story of fear. His waiting at home
is the time when he is getting more and more worried. The account of
what he thought about at home is not one of playing it down: not only
does he say that he thought he was in a pretty bad way, but also getting
worse. Moreover, he indicates that he was not able to identify his ailment
(as he says, explicitly referring to his lack of classical symptoms of
appendicitis). The speaker was wondering, and he was worried about
what was happening to him. The expression 'god only knows...' is
hardly indicative of the speaker's curiosity; rather, it is his fear that
comes through. This is not an instance of stoicism (and thus lack of
emotionality) but an instance of fear. As I shall argue in Chapter 6, one

does not have to use emotion labels in order to construct past emotional experience.

Now, as I said, it might be a dramatised story about being close to death and cheating it, but it is hardly a story of heroism, stoicism and so on. But it is also a story of helplessness. The speaker seems unable to take matters into his own hands. In modern-day Britain, one does not need to wait for one doctor to be admitted to hospital (to all intents and purposes to save one's life). The speaker seems only able to do what he is or will be told, either by the doctor or the receptionist. Judging by the story, it does not bear thinking about what would have happened if the doctor had not come in that evening. Ultimately, I think it is a story of disempowerment, not heroism or stoicism (for further critique of Coates's book, see Kulick, 2003).

Just as with research making claims about men not being in touch with their (positive) emotions, I think that Coates's analysis is hinged upon the assumption of masculine lack of emotionality. The literature and debates on gender and masculinity I mentioned in the previous section are quite enough to disprove any claims about masculinity in general. Who are these unemotional men? What class, ethnicity, age? What circumstances are they in? What contexts are at stake? As Stearns ironically observes, pointing out the untenability of the argument that all men apparently have to do is to look at the female model which 'providentially offers healthy emotionality, true friendship, non-competitive achievement, long life and mental health' (Stearns, 1979:179).

The model of the unemotional man not only grossly oversimplifies but, despite occasional claims to the contrary, essentialises masculinity as well as femininity. In fact, Lutz (1996) proposes that the cultural and academic model of 'unemotional man' is not so much a reflection of suppressing emotions in men but, rather, the creation of the 'emotional woman'. Furthermore, Fischer and Jansz (1995) suggest there are significant similarities in narrated accounts of emotions by men and women, which they link to the cultural model of personhood as the dominant one in such narratives. Most importantly, as I shall show throughout the book, the model simply does not stand up to the empirical data. Edley and Wetherell (1997; see also 1999) reject the notion of the 'retributive man' and prefer to see how men and their identities are constituted in talk, pointing out the 'ideological battlefield' with often contradictory identities, some of them ready to be challenged or suppressed. Particularly at this moment I would like to stress the polemical nature of what follows throughout the book. What I shall be arguing is not only the theoretical implausibility of generalisations about all men in all circumstances but I shall show that in view of the empirical evidence, the models of masculine lack of emotionality (or masculine anything for that matter) are untenable.

My disagreement with those proposing the model of the unemotional man is not merely at the level of its empirical viability, however; it is also at the level of the theoretical approach to masculinity. It is implausible to make a claim about unemotional masculinity precisely because such masculinity does not exist. There is no unemotional or emotional masculinity. If anything, there are locally negotiated masculine identities in which men construct themselves in a particular way. Extrapolating it to masculinity is impossible. I shall not only show that in these local contexts men do speak about their emotions, but I will also show that they do it directly and quite openly and that emotions, also in men's own discourse, can be used to define what men are. As I said in the previous section, I want to offer a much more context-bound insight into masculinity and masculine identity, which is hardly available at the level of all men, at all times, in all circumstances.

Discourse and its analysis

This book is about discourse, about how people talk, and about the linguistic and discursive resources they use. Having noted that identities, including masculinities, are made up of discourse, it is necessary to outline the approach to discourse taken in this book. However, I am not going to offer a comprehensive account of my approach to discourse analysis because I have done that elsewhere recently (Barker and Galasiński, 2001), and the review I offer here is based upon the earlier one. Here, I shall limit myself only to what I think are the most important points.

I am situating my analyses in Critical Discourse Analysis (CDA), although that is not to say that there is a commonly accepted version of it. It is an amalgamation of a number of approaches including French discourse analysis (e.g., Pecheux, 1982); critical linguistics (Fowler *et al.*, 1979; Fowler, 1991; Hodge and Kress, 1993); social semiotics (Hodge and Kress, 1988; Kress and van Leeuwen, 1996); socio-cultural change and change in discourse (Fairclough, 1989, 1992, 1995) and socio-cognitive studies (e.g., van Dijk, 1993, 1998). (For a review of strands within CDA, see Fairclough and Wodak, 1997; Fairclough, 2003.) This chapter is not designed, however, to offer a review of the strands within the CDA (van Dijk 1997); instead I would like to set out a model of discourse analysis with which I have sympathy and which I shall be using throughout this book.

Critical Discourse Analysis

CDA is a textually oriented analysis (Fairclough, 1992), which means that it concerns close analysis of texts, whether written, spoken, or indeed visual (Kress and van Leeuwen, 1996). The focus upon the content and the form of stretches of discourse is the basis of any argument a discourse analyst makes. The focus upon the lexico-grammatical recourses of language – that is, upon the semantics and syntax of an utterance – is complemented by that upon the functions of what is said within the local context, and the social actions thus accomplished.

Below are what I think are the crucial principles of discourse analysis (based on van Dijk, 1997). Studying it in its local and global context, preferably as a constitutive element of the context, I am interested in analysing real-life discourse; it should not be improved or sanitised in any way. I shall consider context as settings, participants and their communicative and social roles, goals, relevant social knowledge, norms and values, institutional or organisational structures.

Discourse is understood as a form of social practice within a socio-cultural context: that is to say, language users are not isolated individuals. They are engaged in communicative activities as members of social groups, organisations, institutions and cultures. To a considerable extent they speak the way one should speak, the way it is appropriate to speak. Moreover, language, discourse and communication are rule-governed activities. They include both strict grammatical rules (what we say is either grammatical or not) and 'softer', more negotiable principles of interaction (J. Thomas, 1995). Discourse analysts are interested not only in language users' following of such rules, but also ways in which they interact with each other (e.g., for stylistic effect), and how they are violated, ignored or suspended (Grice, 1975; Brown and Levinson, 1987).

Locating discourse analysis within its critical strand, I make assumptions as to the character of the analysis. First, following Wodak (1999), the analysis should avoid easy, dichotomous explanations of the phenomena studied. Second, discourse analysts are interested in uncovering contradictions or dilemmas (Billig *et al.*, 1988) underpinning social life. Third, the analysis is self-reflexive. It is impossible to avoid bringing into research and analysis the analyst's values and evaluations. There is no escape from the fact I was born and educated in a Communist country, with a set of gender ideologies, values and daily practices associated with masculinity and used in local constructions of masculine identities. There is no escape from the fact that for a number of years now I have been living as a 'foreigner', identifiable by my accent and other practices as an outsider (for a discussion of reflexivity in research see also Blommaert, 1997; Galasiński, 1997a, b; Verschueren, 1999). However, the linguistic analysis of discourse, anchored within systemic-functional linguistics (Halliday and Hasan, 1985; Halliday, 1994, 1978), can help reduce the arbitrariness of interpretation by anchoring it in the discourse form itself. It is interpretations, and not analyses, that are open, dynamic and imbued with the analyst's perspective. Thus there is not a single ultimately correct interpretation because it is always subject to change (Wodak, 1999).

Now, CDA makes a number of assumptions about discourse.

Discourse is socially constitutive

Discourse, as I said before, is a form of social practice entering into 'dialectical' relationship with the contexts in which they occur: that is to say, discourse is constitutive of and constituted by social and political 'realities' (Fairclough and Wodak, 1997; van Leeuwen and Wodak, 1999).

Discourse is a system of options

The socially constitutive view of discourse is tightly related to the assumption that discourse is a system of options from which language users make their choices (Chouliaraki, 1998). The construction of any representation of 'reality' is necessarily selective, entailing decisions as to which aspects of that reality to include and how to arrange them. Each selection carries its share of socially ingrained values so that representation is socially constructed (Hodge and Kress, 1993; Hall, 1997) and alternative representations are not only always possible, but they carry divergent significance and consequences (Fowler, 1996). Nevertheless, texts seek to impose a 'preferred reading' (Hall, 1981) or 'structure of faith' (Menz, 1989) upon the addressee.

Following work in social semiotics, I shall view representation as a process subject to regimes of production and reception that are implicated in the ideological complexes of social formations. Practices of representation, resting on more or less contested cultural classifications of people and circumstances, are always part of a communicative situation marked by, and indicative of, the power relations between communicators and the subjects of representation (Hodge and Kress, 1988; Kress and van Leeuwen, 1996; Hall, 1997).

Discourse is ideological

The selective character of representation leads to the view that it is through discourse and other semiotic practices that ideologies are formulated, reproduced and reinforced. I understand the term 'ideology' as social (general and abstract) representations shared by members of a group and used by them to accomplish everyday social practices: acting and communicating (Fowler, 1985; Billig *et al.*, 1988; van Dijk, 1998).

These representations are organised into systems which are deployed by social classes and other groups 'in order to make sense of, figure out and render intelligible the way society works' (Hall, 1996:26), while at the same time they are capable of 'ironing out' the contradictions, dilemmas and antagonisms of practices in ways which accord with the interests and projects of power (Chouliaraki and Fairclough, 1999).

For Billig and his associates (1988), discourse is a site of power struggle in which ideologies implicated by discursive choices are the subject of struggles for dominance within and between social groups. One of the ideologically relevant discourse structures pointed to by van Dijk (1998:209) is interaction and, more specifically, the realm of interactional control. Who starts the exchange, who ends it, who initiates new topics, who interrupts whom, and so on, may all be indicative of the interlocutor's power and as such is ideologically charged. Highlighting relations of power in societies, CDA, along with cultural studies, argues that ideologies are discursive in character.

The ideological nature of discourse does not mean that ideology can be simply 'read off' texts by analysts (a criticism frequently made against the critical linguistics strand within CDA; e.g., Fairclough 1992); rather, discourse can be seen to accomplish ideologies (Billig *et al.*, 1988; see also Billig 1990a, b) while not being equated with them (van Dijk, 1998).

Text is multifunctional

Texts are products of speaking or writing so that the discursive practices with which I am engaged whilst writing this book are presented to readers as 'text'. One of the main assumptions about text that we make is that it is multifunctional. This assumption flows from the direct association of Critical Discourse Analysis with systemic and functional linguistics, most particularly that of Halliday (1978, 1994). There are three such functions: ideational, interpersonal, textual.

It is through the *ideational* function of language that texts are able to refer to realities 'outside' (or indeed 'inside') speakers, enabling them to render intelligible their experience of the world. The cornerstone of the ideational function is related to what Halliday calls transitivity. It is transitivity that enables the representation in multiple ways of an implied extra-linguistic reality. The two main elements of transitivity by which 'reality' can be rendered intelligible are 'process' and 'participant':

that is, in terms of what happens or is the case (process), and by or to whom (participant). This can be complemented by the third element: circumstances.

The *interpersonal* function refers to the ability of language users to interact with each other. It means that through language speakers can set up social relationships with their addressees. Thus, by giving an order, speakers assume their right to do so, and by issuing a promise, they commit themselves to doing something. Moreover, by addressing each other in a particular way, controlling access to the floor or certain communicative acts, the interpersonal function of language performs a variety of tasks related to how speakers position themselves with regard to their audiences. The interpersonal function is also responsible for rendering the speaker's attitude to what someone says: how certain they are in saying something, how committed they are to it, or whether they distance themselves from their attitudes. Alternatively, speakers may adopt particular speech roles with regard to their utterances (e.g., author, spokesperson or mouthpiece).

Finally, language serves a *textual* function by which some of its elements are responsible for making discourse appear 'as text' while signalling its relevance to the context in which it appears. The textual function of language makes it intelligible to the addressee precisely as a text that makes sense within itself and within the context of its appearance. It is important to stress that text as a whole is multifunctional and normally serves all three functions at the same time. The textual function is also responsible for arranging information in what is said or written: which element of the clause is positioned as known, given, and which is telling us something new, unknown.

Text is intertextual

Finally, CDA assumes intertextuality of texts. It refers to the quality of texts, as Fairclough (1992:84) puts it, which are 'full of snatches of other texts, which may be explicitly demarcated or merged in, and which the text may assimilate, contradict, ironically echo, and so forth'. Thus intertextuality signals the accumulation and generation of meaning across texts where all meanings depend on other meanings.

Discourse analysis involves a constant self-reflexive trade-off between the researcher's interests, values and knowledge of the context against the practicalities of a microanalysis that cannot go on indefinitely. CDA is carried out in two stages. The first one, the analysis proper, concerns itself with 'hard' data, its linguistic and discursive form while the second stage of the analysis is the interpretation of the findings of stage one.

The first stage should be seen as quite independent of the analyst (providing that one accepts lexico-grammatical analysis as valid and quasi-objective within the cultural context of its use) in that it is repeatable and empirically verifiable. Thus, when we ask ourselves about the thematic structure of the clauses of a text, the answers are likely to be quite similar regardless of the analyst. The results of such an analysis (given a fixed definition of the grammatical terms such as 'theme' and 'rheme') can be disputed only in very complex cases, which means that interpretation, however contentious and ideologically motivated, follows on from an empirically verifiable analysis of the text. That is to say, interpretative analysis comes after the phenomena in the text structure have been observed and analysed linguistically.

It is in this context that I see my critique of an extract from Coates's book above. My rejection of her argument that the extract is about heroism and proposal that it should be interpreted in terms of power-lessness is underpinned by my contention that Coates ignored the linguistic/discursive structure of the data so that the interpretation, while always political, becomes not much more than a political exercise. What I propose is at least the deferral of the political into the stage which is secondary to the analytic stage.

Overview of the book

My primary focus in this book is men's narratives of their emotions. I want to approach them from two perspectives. On the one hand, I am interested in how emotions are used to construct masculinities and, on the other, in the discursive strategies which are used by men when they talk about their emotional experience. I shall see these constructions and strategies as resulting from negotiations of the local contextual concerns with the society's discourses on men and gender. But at the same time I am bracketing off the issue concerning to what extent they are indicative of masculine power, its mechanisms and, more generally, power relations between genders.

The data I am going to use in the book come predominantly from a research project into individual perceptions and public representations of middle age (in Chapter 6 I shall use data from another project which I shall describe there).[1] The informants were men and women over the age of 40, and thus either currently experiencing middle age (40–60) or talking about it retrospectively (60+). All the men were white English heterosexuals, coming from different social classes (with occupation used as a proxy for class), living in the Birmingham and Black Country area of the United Kingdom. Most of them either had been or were in stable relationships with partners (usually wives). The interviews concerned a variety of issues related to middle age itself, the experience of its onset, and its relation to family and working relationships. The final corpus of interview data obtained consisted of interviews with 55 individuals (26 male, 29 female) lasting between 50 and 100 minutes (average duration around 60 minutes).

In Chapter 2 I begin the exploration of the first perspective of the book. I am interested in the use of emotion narratives in constructions of masculinity. I shall demonstrate that, despite the apparently prevalent stereotype of unemotional masculinity, men construct both themselves, as well as masculinity in general, in terms of emotions. In addition, I shall show that in women's narratives too, masculinity can be seen as emotional.

Chapters 3 and 4 change the perspective to that of an exploration of ways in which men speak about their emotions. In Chapter 3, I shall explore two main strategies used in the narratives analysed. First, I shall examine distancing strategies, such as those in which emotional states are not ascribed directly to those who are constructed as experiencing them. Second, I shall be interested in their counterpart: accounts in which men directly ascribe emotional states to themselves. I shall also propose an account of the social functions of the two strategies. In Chapter 4, I shall investigate the fact that men frequently denied having certain emotions and will argue that these stories also contribute to the image of the emotional man. I shall argue that such narratives indicate a certain 'emotional competence' on men's part.

In Chapters 5 and 6, I shall narrow the focus of my inquiry and explore how men talk about their emotions as part of some particular experiences they had. Thus, in Chapter 5 I shall discuss the way men talk about fatherhood and how they relate fatherhood to emotionality. I shall also show that men's constructions of emotional fatherhood are seconded by those made by women. In Chapter 6, I shall discuss the ways in which Polish men talk about unemployment and focus on the construction of helplessness in men's narratives. On the basis of such constructs, I shall be arguing that emotions do not need to be constructed with the use of lexical labels naming them: grammatical resources of language can also be utilised to construct emotional experience.

In the concluding chapter I shall not only review the book's arguments, but I shall also consider the relationship of 'emotion talk' to the performance of masculinity and offer some comment upon the frequently met contention about omnirelevance of gender in interaction.

Note

1. The project was designed by John Benson and myself and funded by the Leverhulme Trust, which I would like gratefully to acknowledge.

2
Stories of Emotional Masculinity

Living emotions

In a research concerning women's (re-)negotiation of gender roles in post-Communist Poland,[1] when asked about her views on the 'position' of the head of the family, one of the interviewed women replied as follows.

Extract 1
BR, female, born 1955

> BR: (...) men.... were the first to lose their jobs, least of, secondly they are like big children, they have no character at all, they break down completely, it would be best if they were allowed they would hang themselves and the problem would be gone. They weep a lot, they complain much and they do little, but want a lot of fuss around it, big time. They are impractical. I can't see them, maybe in the past, when there were these caves, and he went with the spear and caught the animal, for free, so the woman could hunt it, but now it has got flatter big time. and here life is now a jungle, battle to survive. They just do not fit in. Maybe they would fit in the jungle, but absolutely not the urban one. Women are more practical and smarter. That's what I have said.
>
> I: [laughter] and what's it like in your family?
>
> BR: that's what I said, as above, exactly, exactly the same.

What is striking about this statement is not merely the complete reversal of stereotypical masculinity, but also the speaker's total lack of hesitation in making it. The stereotypical and academic models of masculinity have been dismissed in one move. The helpless men are juxtaposed with practical women who manage to survive in the urban jungle. Linguistically, they are constructed as agents in activities such as crying, while their bread-winning activities are limited to catching animals, with connotations of luck rather than strategy. It is women who are possessed of strategy and skill and thus can be the real hunters. It seems men are not even capable of taking their own lives, because they wait for permission which is unlikely to come.

Moreover, BR's words, with implicit reference to the period of post-Communism (the reference to men's job losses), could also be seen as a 'lived' version of the historicity of masculinity. Although, obviously, she does not make the point explicitly, she does imply that the change of socio-economic conditions has had an adverse impact upon men and, by implication, masculinity.

Men cry, men break down; they have no spine, no character. It is the woman who seems to be the foundation upon which the weakling man can lean. The version of masculinity the interviewed woman proposes in her utterance runs counter to just about all its models. One could of course dismiss it as a token-utterance, completely uncharacteristic of the 'discourse of masculinity'. One could also seek an explanation of the very strong opinions shown in this extract in the fact that BR is the main bread-winner in her family. However, I would like to argue that, in fact, it is BR's version of masculinity which is closer to the complex lived model conveyed by both men and women in their narratives. It is also a version of masculinity that can be constructed by men themselves.

What I would like to show in this chapter is that despite the frequently encountered association of masculinity with rationality, self-discipline and distancing from emotions or emotionality, the data I shall present offer a significantly more complex picture of the relationship between masculinity and emotions. There were many narratives in which masculinity was in fact constructed in terms of emotionality, and they did not contain the 'negative'[2] emotions suggested by such theorists as Hearn (1993). Rather, both men and masculinity are constructed in terms of a number of emotions, sometimes explicitly targeted at people, sometimes not. The stereotype of the 'unemotional man' showing itself in public and also probably in private discourses of masculinity must be doubted as regards its pervasiveness in discourses which are not explicitly focusing upon men in general, masculinity or gender. Alternatively, some speakers constructed emotions as parallel, not related to gender or masculinity in particular, but still made no attempts at constructing masculinity as unemotional or free of emotionality.

My discussion in this chapter will take the following route. First, I shall show how the interviewed men constructed themselves, as individuals in terms of emotions or emotionality. Second, I shall demonstrate how their narratives constructed men and masculinity generally in such terms, occasionally situating emotionality as unrelated to gender. Finally, I shall present some narratives offered by the female interviewees and show also that women's narratives of masculinity, just like BR's above, are not free from associations with emotionality.

Individual men and their emotions

There are a number of ways in which the interviewed men spoke about their emotions and related them to their masculinity. Speakers constructed their emotionality as an all-encompassing dimension of their lives, or as something relevant only in a particular sphere, at different levels of explicitness.

Extract 2
CG, male, born 1913, lines 77–96

> I: can you tell me in a bit more detail about what your life was like in this span – you know – your years between forty or sixty, is there maybe a particular point in that part of your adulthood when you were around forty when you would feel a new phase of your life was starting?

> CG: yes I can ((clears throat)) because (.) one thing of the legacy of my parents separating and my going away for school was that I suffered from very great insecurity – as I suspect lots and lots of people do – I think I had an inferiority complex. and although I always talked a lot I was in fact very shy. I used to worry terribly (.) what people thought of me. I think a great advantage of reaching middle age if you are a reasonably balanced person is that you begin to get all these problems into perspective. You cease to care so much what people think of you. you become your own master. and I've been very fortunate since I've suddenly realised that if people don't like me – well although I – I like to be liked – unless I've done something wrong to deserve their dislike I don't worry about it.

Extract 3
NI, male, born 1953, lines 288–98

> I: So is there anything you've stopped doing because you felt you were getting too old for it? NI: No. I'm a bit slower, I'm more cautious. if I go

out for a big walk in the mountains now I plan it a bit more. I pace myself a bit easier. I make sure I've got plenty to drink and plenty to eat. and a – and I watch ((unclear)) I plan more what I'm doing I know exactly what I'm doing. I know where my escape routes are ((laughs)). and I think when I was younger I didn't care you know ((slight laugh)). I think I care more now I'm older.

Both men define themselves in terms of their emotions, CG in terms of past ones, NI in terms of the present. Moreover, both informants seem to be aware that their emotional dispositions changed over the years: CG has stopped worrying, stopped being shy, and NI has started caring (whatever that might actually mean). There is no attempt to hedge, to qualify their statements about emotions. CG seems not to have a problem with defining a significant period of his life in terms of fear, whilst NI seems happy to talk about himself in, shall I say, 'softer' terms.

Significantly for my argument here, both men are not merely relating some short-term emotional outbursts; rather they describe themselves, the way they were or are, with the questions notably *not* focusing upon emotions. CG sees his emotions in terms of an inferiority complex (something akin to a personality trait). In contrast, CG's current life-stage is marked by the absence of the emotions he spoke about. Denying a particular emotion, as I shall argue in Chapter 4, is also a way of positioning oneself in terms of emotionality. Moreover, CG's successful management of the problem is not down to his strength, hard work, let alone masculinity. Interestingly, putting the problem into perspective is rendered by the impersonal 'you'. The informant talks about the course of things, rather than about his own achievements. Somewhat similarly in the case of NI's narrative, his caring is put down to his being older, to chronology, rather than to working on himself.

Constructing a period of life, or life in general, in terms of emotions occurs quite frequently in my corpus, as witness the following examples.

Extract 4
TE, male, born 1950, lines 452–61

I: Ehm what would you say are the most important things to you in your current phase of life?

TE: (. . .) Enjoying yourself. I think if you don't enjoy it I mean that's – you can't force yourself. I mean it – I don't mean you mustn't work at anything 'cus you've got the satisfaction of doing things. it does take work which ehm (. .). yeah yeah – I just – enjoy yourself be true to yourself.

ehm (...). do what I enjoy yeah. ehm (...). yeah that's it really yeah ((slight laugh)).

Extract 5
CG, male, born 1930, lines 885–90

CG: I apologise if I appeared smug during ((the interview)). I'm so happy. and I have been so lucky, I have had a very happy life. and that's been partly dependent on the fact that I have three super kids, good marriage, an interesting job, never a shortage of money – I have no excuse to be resentful about age.

The beginning of TE's story of enjoyment is rendered in impersonal terms. It is as if the speaker was not merely speaking about himself and his desire to enjoy himself in his mid-years. He offers a recipe for middle age: one should enjoy oneself. It is of course difficult to argue here that TE is speaking of men only: the recipe is more for people in general, rather than for men like or unlike him. But it is interesting since, as I shall show shortly, men do construct their emotionality both in contrast to as well as on a par with women's. So TE proposes that people – regardless of their gender – should simply enjoy themselves. This, in turn, is the basis upon which he situates his own enjoyment at the end of his turn. His *joie de vivre*, the 'positive' emotions towards life, seem to be parallel to his masculinity, being in no conflict with it.

CG's self-elicited account is more one of taking stock of his life and he does it in terms of emotions. Even though CG's account focuses on happiness, it is also negative in that the speaker rejects what he perceives as negative emotions, such as being resentful about his age. It is only the 'positive' emotions which are or should be part of his view of the world and life. Emotionality is also mentioned as natural, or perhaps encountered in certain aspects of male life. One of them, perhaps surprisingly, given gender stereotypes, is the physical appearance of men.

Extract 6
DQ, male, born 1957, lines 899–918

I: If you see something like stop hair loss or – dyeing your hair that would – wouldn't you be?

DQ: No, no my immediate reaction to that is how sad really if it's just something that ehm if – if I got (..) overly concerned about my white moustache the very simple thing to do would be to shave it off.

I: Have you been thinking about that?

DQ: Ehm (.) it occurred to me once or twice (.) when it started to white over the last 12 months really noticeably (.) and ehm I'm thinking to myself you know – you are looking older ehm as I say it's interesting that something like a moustache probably gives the impression of age and when you're younger you perhaps want to look older but when you're getting older ((laughs)) it might be worth shaving it off ((laughs)). I don't know it (.) I'm not obsessed with having to look younger I'm quite happy really ((quiet)) it's not something that overly worries me.

lines 938–54

I: Do you observe people of your age who you kind of think are behaving in this ridiculous way?

DQ: Ehm (. . .) I – I haven't noticed. If – if somebody was doing something like that I would pick up on it certainly (. .) I can – I can remember somebody that I used to work with up to 10 years ago who – who (.) wore this – full wig who was obviously totally bald and wore a wig. And it – it was – you just had to stop yourself from staring at it really ((laughs)). It's just not something that I could ehm (.) countenance ever. Basically and yet this guy felt that he'd got this problem and yet now the (.) the – the fashion really is that is to shave the head. Why worry about being (.) bald? Why worry about it? Ehm but being fair-skinned I find that (. .) it is a difficulty in – in the summer so I burn. And it hurts ((laughs)). And I've got quite a few straw hats ((laughs)).

Extract 7
NE, male, born 1949, lines 714–23

I: do people comment on how old you look?

NE: well! no not directly, but I have been ehm confused for my daughter's grandfather. ((laughs)) which is a bit un- ((unclear)) I do find that upsetting. I do find that upsetting! ((laughs)) because you – again you know you don't – you don't actually feel as if you're (.) I mean I think of grandfathers as being in their mid-sixties you know. but I mean obviously that doesn't have to be the case. so I think that – that probably ehm (.) that's the one time that, eh

DQ in both his responses constructs physical appearance as something which is or can be worrying. In the first utterance, he implies being concerned, but not overly concerned, about looking older in his moustache. A bit further on in the interview, he implies a general principle of men being worried about going bald. His example of a colleague who wore a wig suggests that he had gone too far in pretending not to have gone bald, rather than that he is just a token man who worries about such things. DQ's rhetorical question of why worry about getting bald is an indication that men worry about going bald (another trait of emotional masculinity, it seems).

In extract 7, NE does not attempt to construct such a general principle; instead he talks about instances of being taken as belonging to the generation of his father, something that upset him. Note that the narrative of having the strong emotion is anchored within a narrative which implies his strong emotional attitude towards the issue, but despite that he does not use emotive language (Ochs and Schieffelin, 1989; Caffi and Janney, 1994). His hesitations and repairs lead to a very jagged account, suggesting – as Meinhof originally proposed (Meinhof, 1997; see also Galasiński and Meinhof, 2002) – unresolved issues in the speaker's life-story, which render his protestation about not feeling a grandfather emotional.

Emotionality, however, is not only associated with the private sphere of men's lives. The next extract shows an interesting involvement of emotions in men's professional activities.

Extract 8
SD, male, born 1922, lines 494–513

> I: for yourself, are there – can you remember any changes, how you might have changed from when you were young or in your early adulthood to when you got older, how your views on life or on politics or your values changed or remained the same during –
>
> SD: well they obviously changed. it would be dreadful if they remained static wouldn't it, it'd be like an idiot then ((laughs)). yes, obviously change. (.) things happened and eh (.) you look at things in a different light, obviously as you get older because you've got that much experience of life. ((inhales and talks)) (.) and I think being in the probation service was the – best thing I ever did. it was a ((unclear)) having concern for people. ((unclear)) you wouldn't be a probation officer if you didn't have a concern for people and their problems. (.) ehm (..) you learned a lot about other people and how they see life. (..) it was a worthwhile job. very demanding, long hours. (.) at the end of the day you thought: well – (at least) it's been a useful day.

Despite SD's rendering of his emotions with the use of distancing strategies – he is speaking of 'having' an emotion and uses the impersonal 'you', rather than using a direct reference to himself (see Chapter 3) – still he associates his profession with a certain emotional ability, 'a concern for others'. As before, the utterance could also be seen as 'emotional' in the sense of not only describing someone who is concerned, but also constructing the speaker as 'empathetic' with others.

I would like to finish this section of this chapter by discussing another two aspects of the narratives. First, the informants constructed, in more or less general terms, emotional masculinity in contrast to unemotional femininity. Second, they also positioned masculinity as parallel to emotionality, in that masculinity and its traits had nothing to do with emotions. As the speaker in extract 10 shows, he may well feel emotions, but they have nothing to do with emotionality, or indeed the masculine stereotype he draws upon.

First, however, we have another extract.

Extract 9
II, male, born 1918, lines 722–45

II: There are certain things I would like to alter about my middle age yes. if I had the opportunity. but I know I shan't get that opportunity so I don't worry about it ((laughs)). I try to ehm guide even my sons as old as they are, I – I try to guide them and say you know, I don't think you should do things that way but I would not tell them not to do anything. I can only sort of hint. as I say I'm very fortunate. my sons are very good and my family are very good. I know so many families who have problems that I feel so very very fortunate. I have a friend ehm who lived in ((place name)) she's now living in ((place name)) and after – we were friends before my wife died and before her husband died because we went to the same what we – you would call church. and ehm after our spouses died we started to realise that we could go and do things together which we couldn't do when my wife and her husband were alive because we had to deal with them and look after them. like go on a bus – a bus ride, 'cus we get a free bus pass in ((place name)). so couldn't go on a bus ride, we couldn't go on to concerts to symphony hall, I mean we enjoy that. ehm so for the last few years we became quite good friends and talking of good friends that's the only good friend I've really ever had. ehm but her family's completely different to mine. she found it very strange this closeness of my family (. . .)

After a description of his contentment with his family, II switches to talking about his female friend and constructs her as surprised by the emotional bond in his family. It is as if the gender stereotypes were reversed and it is the woman who is within the family with emotional problems, the state of affairs she (by implication) considers normal, and thus is surprised by the emotional closeness of the speaker's family. Interestingly, the juxtaposition of the genders comes quite naturally within the narrative, precisely after the account of the interviewer's bond with his sons.

Consider also the following extract in which the informant is talking about his experiences of becoming a single father.

Extract 10
KI, male, born 1933, lines 523–65

I: didn't you feel lonely when you were suddenly on your own again?

(.)

KI: not really. (.) not really because I've always had lots of friends. and I mean you don't – these change evolve slowly. so you don't say oh eighteen you don't say ((whistles)) ps! she's gone! that's it. I got nothing on. I mean from say sixteen (.) well (..) ehm I didn't – (.) I didn't have the problems of ensuring that she got the right clothes, for instance. and my son hadn't got the right clothes. it's really very difficult for a man to start thinking of children's clothes. and all the things that children want. and (..) and all the funny things that happen to girls. at times. and (.) and (.) I have (.) I have a memory of my daughter and uff I feel so bad about it now. I didn't really understand at the time and I- I don't know whether she thinks about it. I don't know whether she is- ah I came home (.) I tell you I'm getting very personal there (.) came home one night and (.) she was in bed. and- well she went to bed. and when I went up to see her, she was in tears, crying. and (.) I was furious for some reason or other. I was absolutely fuming, lost my temper with her. I said what's the matter with you? what you're crying for? and ((slight laugh)) she'd – she'd just started her periods and she didn't really, you know – and I was absolutely (.) jumping. because I said come on then – basically ((unclear)) every woman in the world has these, you know, what the hell are you crying for! well over the years various girls have said to me it's a (.) ehm it's a time in a girl's life that is quite ((unclear)) and I (.) regret that time, or that moment very very very much. I really really do. because it wasn't until you know you start talking to people. that some girls find this – well being a man I don't know about these things. and eh ((laughs)) having to go round the chemist's for her on occasions and just. (.) it's just one of these things, so how a woman gets on. a woman – I think with a woman – I think for a start you don't have that problem with a boy. so to some extent, to some extent, a woman left on her own with children is far able to cope more easily than a man is. I couldn't do that again. I could never ever do that again.

Before continuing, I would like to make a more general note on this fragment. It seems to me that this kind of narrative can quite easily be used to construct models of masculinity associated with violent emotions. What we have here is a man explicitly speaking about his anger, fury, or 'jumping', as he put it. What I shall be arguing, however, is that the narrative can be problematised and not taken as a straightforward reference to masculine violence or 'negative' emotions.

Here, I am particularly interested in the speaker's overt positioning of himself as a man. He offers quite a lucid and emotional account of his emotional outburst. Quite interestingly, KI is not using the stereotype of masculinity to account for his anger, his regret or even his emotional unpreparedness for being a single father. Rather, he chooses to evoke his masculinity as a means of justifying being unprepared to deal with what he perceives as female problems, or a female area of life: the onset of his daughter's menstruation, or finding the right clothes for his children. His emotions, constructed outside masculinity, are to do with his relationship with his daughter and his lack of understanding of the problem he was faced with. And it is only the lack of understanding that is positioned as having to do with his masculinity. The beginning of the frame introducing the story of the emotional outburst – *I tell you I'm getting very personal there* – could, perhaps, be seen as an indication of the awareness of a man that he is beginning to tell a story full of his own emotion, an implicit presence of the stereotype of the unemotional man in KI's narrative. I do not think, however, that such an interpretation would be warranted. It is more plausible in my opinion to see the interjection as the speaker's awareness that he is letting the interviewer, a stranger, in on a family secret, and feels some discomfort because of it. The invocation of masculinity used to justify the outburst and reinforce the regret is, again, not constructed in terms of emotions: it is, rather, the continuation of the initial claim to man's incompetence.

KI's construction of his emotions lies in parallel to his construction of masculinity. Masculinity might have something to do with difficulties in becoming a single father, in bringing up children, but not with emotionality. Moreover, the emotionality KI invokes is not merely a 'negative' one: KI speaks of his anger, but at the same time speaks of his emotional attitude towards the event, especially his regret because of it.

Masculinity and its emotions

In this section I shall be interested in the ways the interviewed men constructed masculinity in general. As previously, also masculinity in general can be and is constructed in terms of emotionality. The first two extracts show men speaking of masculinity and fatherhood in generic terms. They position them in terms of emotions.

Extract 11
CG, male, born, 1930, lines 26–37

> CG: (. . .) I think one only feels your physical years when you're not well. now when I'm ill (.) I get ehm I feel sorry for myself like all men do and I may well feel older. when I'm well I'm sure that my mental approach is no different now than it was thirty years ago. eh I enjoy immensely being with young people. (.) All my life I've been teased and I enjoy being teased. and I think and hope I can truthfully say I've never taken myself very seriously. (.) I feel sorry for people who do take themselves seriously. because that is the most (.) devastatingly single point that age has been. I think I even sometimes see people who are old at thirty by taking themselves so seriously.

Extract 12
KI, male, born 1933, lines 507–21

> I: and how old were you when your daughter left home?
>
> KI: she left home – was it 36 – she left home eighteen years ago.
>
> I: mmh. so how did you feel when she left home?
>
> KI: ((exhales)) puh! exhausted. no (.) I felt relief really. if the truth isn't ((unclear)) from the fact that I didn't have to (.) think about it, about all the things about girls and what they get up to and what they don't get up to (.) I didn't have to worry about that. 'cause I think a father worries more about his daughter than possibly the mother would. I don't know, I don't know, I don't really know. [. . .]

There is no hint of the stereotype of the unemotional or angry man in CG's account. He uses masculinity, or rather masculine emotionality, to justify feeling sorry for himself by positioning it as a normal characteristic of all men. All men feel sorry for themselves when they are unwell. If anything, one could postulate the existence of the stereotype of the whingeing man. But even though CG probably does not like feeling sorry for himself, the problem for him, importantly, is not emotionality. He is quite happy to continue talking about his emotions. It is that particular emotion – feeling sorry for oneself – that is the problem, yet there is no attempt to cast the emotion as 'un-masculine' or anything of the sort. On the contrary, CG seems to accept his masculine nature. In extract 12, in turn, KI explicitly juxtaposes fatherhood with motherhood, and it is fathers who seem to be more caring towards daughters. There are two stages in which this positioning is done: first, in negative terms, the daughter's leaving home relieves KI of 'having to' worry about her. The construction is very important here: fatherly worry about his daughter seems to be a necessity, something natural. It is only the daughter's leaving that relieved him of the duty; he cannot do it himself. And indeed, the naturalness of the worrying is reinforced by, second, the generic reference to fathers. I shall come back to this extract in Chapter 5.

The following extract shows emotional masculinity more implicitly. Moreover, probably because of the generation of the informant, it refers to emotionality between men only.

Extract 13
CL, male, born 1922, lines 700–14

> I: that's interesting. (.) so would you say that (.) living through the war at that young age has – has influenced your – has had an impact on your outlook on life in general?
>
> CL: I think so yes to a degree. ehm (..) I think those who (.) saw military service (..) are to some extent slightly a race apart from everybody else. (.) just to an extent. and that is why I think there's eh – (.) I've still got (.) many friends who I made at Cambridge, when I went back. because there is this (.) well we don't talk about it, I mean there is a hidden bond (.) you know we were the lucky ones, we came home eh (.) and eh we've a lot to be thankful for and ehm (.) so to that extent I think. yes it has. I mean it doesn't affect one in one's day-to-day (.) living or – in any way.

The hidden bond which the informant refers to is, I think, a reference to some deep emotional link between him and some other men (a link quite in contrast with the majority of analyses of male friendships in Nardi, 1992). CL taps into a myth of what might be referred to as 'brotherhood in arms'. The examples from literature and film, or popular culture in general, are numerous, with representations of the Second World War or the Vietnam War being the most obvious and fruitful examples. Needless to say, society keeps its highest accolades for those who care enough for others to either sacrifice their lives or put themselves in life-threatening danger. In this reference to popular culture, I do not mean, however, the exploits visually rendered by movies with Arnold Schwarzenegger, Sylvester Stallone or, more recently, Mel Gibson. It is not about macho heroism. Rather, I mean the deep emotional commitment to the fallen other that leads to sacrifice. In Hollywood terms, it is much more *Forrest Gump* or *Saving Private Ryan* than the likes of *First Blood*.

This is indeed what I think the informant is talking about. I do not believe that the silence he speaks of is a reference to men's inability to feel, or to talk about things. The mutual emotional involvement is still implicit and taken for granted and is very much part of the experience of utmost trauma and thus perhaps does not need to be spoken about. Inferring from such a statement some general inability of men to speak about their deep emotional involvement with each other does not make sense. One does not need to say anything to communicate as numerous studies on silence have shown (see, e.g., Jaworski, 1993). Importantly, the silence the speaker refers to applies only to the discourse of the friends (clearly, he does speak about the bond to the interviewer), and it draws upon a deep assumption to the emotional bond. Does one need to spell out things if one takes them for granted, we could ask.

The next three extracts show again the gender-free constructions of emotions. Thus the changing emotions have nothing to do with masculinity, despite the informant's positioning himself in such terms (extract 14). Alternatively, emotions may have to do with people, rather than men, and it is as people rather than as men that the informants occasionally chose to position themselves (extracts 15 and 16).

The gender-free account of emotionality in the next example is turned into an account of the changing husband–wife relationship. The narrated changes of emotionality are explicitly linked to aspects other than masculinity, despite the interviewee adopting the subject role of a man.

Extract 14
WC, male, born 1926, lines, 687–714

> WC1: (. . .) I suppose what does happen, you become a bit more benign as you get older.

I: more benign?

WC2: yeah you – you don't – (.) like I suppose when I was younger I was more hot-tempered and things like that and you know and we didn't suffer fools gladly. whereas you get older, your temper is a bit – you know which I think is a natural thing.

I: do you have a particular experience in mind which makes you say that?

WC3: ((clears throat)) no I think it's in general. (I think) what (. .) what used to really annoy me was people – people who were late and things like that, and eh – you know I was trained years ago in the marines that to be punctual is to be five minutes before time. and I've always been like this. now if anyone is late eh (.) I get very uptight, especially with my wife. my wife is always late cause she couldn't – she can't handle time. now (.) I can get a bit uptight about that. and I did, I always did but I'm not too bad at all now. I'm sort of – I'm very relaxed and when she is late she is late. you know? we'll either get there in time or we won't? full stop. whereas before I would be jumping up and down and all that sort of thing ((laughs)).

The interviewee begins with a gender-free account of his 'hot temper', as he puts it. There is no hint in his narrative that he is referring to himself as a man or positioning himself in roles that imply masculinity. Instead, he is speaking with a gender-free subject position, as a person, rather than as a man. Moreover, he explicitly links the changes in his emotionality to age. It is only when he is asked to exemplify what he was saying that he implicitly takes on the role of a man/husband. The references to the relationship with his wife, as well as his marines experience (WC3), position the informant quite clearly as a masculine subject. But the most interesting aspect of the narrative is that the interviewee explicitly talks about the changes in his emotionality. Despite being a man in his narrative, he realises he is no longer so hot-tempered, he does not get that uptight about his wife's lateness. And, finally, all these changes are not about his being a man; rather, they are about him being older. There is no hint that he changed in any other way than his age. His emotions are not to do with his masculinity.

One could, of course, wonder to what extent WC is referring to changes in his masculinity, rather than merely to age. But this kind of reading, I think, would mean making precisely the kind of assumptions that I am trying to counter in this book. It is impossible to make such an argument without making the assumption of some essential quality of masculinity that in one way or another disappears with age; in other words, without the assumption that older men are less manly than younger ones, thereby linking masculinity to, shall I say, 'prime age' and in the process to biology. In other words, we would need to assume that speaking as a man of his age, he necessarily constructs himself as a different man, not just an older one, a different kind of man, so to speak. Given that there is no evidence for such an interpretation in the narrative, such assumptions for me, shall I be so brave as to say, as a balding man, seem quite problematic. They are not, however, particularly surprising in today's developed societies. The cover story of the Polish edition of *Newsweek* (20 July 2003, issue 29) is devoted to men and their health and well-being, including problems related to ageing. The image on the cover shows a man's face which on its left hand side is visibly young, and on its right hand side is visibly old, with grey head hair and eyebrows and wrinkles. The caption under the image says: 'To keep masculinity' (Polish *Zatrzymać męskość*). Worrying as it is, it seems that older men are not men, or perhaps not real men (also Hollander, 2001).

Finally in this section, I would like to show a couple of extracts in which emotionality is not related to masculinity, but rather to humanity.

Extract 15
CL, male, born 1922, lines 1,123–34

I: and have you ever worried about getting older?

CL: no. (.) I mean what is there to worry about? ((laughs)) there are only two certain things in this life: death and taxes, as you ((laughs)) (.) no I think some people do, I suppose some – well some people do worry like that, I've never really worried about getting old. I mean I think it – you know (.) when you are old inevitably you worry about your health and (.) you see friends struck down with those ghastly things. and you – you do worry from time to time and wonder what's gonna happen to you. no but that's as far as it goes.

Extract 16
CG, male, 1930, lines 108–29

I: no no – you know when you were saying you know I was asking is there a particular point in your life when you felt that something

CG: ah! yes saying if that's the point that I would pinpoint. yeah I think it was something that dawned on me (.) fairly slowly (.) ehm (. . .) I think people are of two kinds (.) if they're sensitive they do care what people think of them. if they are thick-skinned and insensitive they tend not to care. I think the latter type of person has an advantage initially because it must be comfortable going through life, particularly when you're young, not being concerned with the impression they are creating. But I think they'll lose out in the end. I think I have come to my own when I'm able to enjoy the company of people without having to do things just to please them. I please myself, I hope in the process I'll please them as well. (...) I think I arrived at that mainly through talking about it with ((wife)). because we're very similar in that respect. We're both – we're both – I can't say shy – retired people. ((wife)) is a bit more (.) withdrawn than I am but then she is extrovert as well. We're both extrovert.

Neither man makes a distinction between men and women when they talk about emotions, one worrying about the ageing process, the other about being thick-skinned (caring or not caring about one's image, which I take to refer to relationships people enter). While CL talks about friends being struck down, once again not specifying their gender, CG positions himself and indeed his wife in a group of those who are sensitive. Implicitly, he constructs two groups of mixed gender. The kind of emotional attitudes or abilities he talks about clearly cross the gender line.

Women's view

At the beginning of this chapter I discussed an extract from a woman's narrative in which she described men in terms of emotions, as weaklings, as people who are unable to cope with the difficulties posed by the life around them. Her narrative was made from the position of a strong woman whose husband was considerably less successful than herself, and was anchored in the deep political and economic changes in Poland, resulting, among other things, in large unemployment, especially in traditionally industrial regions of Poland. In what follows, however, I would like to invoke a larger female perspective on men's emotionality. I want to show that similarly to men themselves, women also construct men as emotional. First, I shall show extracts in which women talk about individual men, then ones in which informants construct their emotions on a par with men's and, finally, an extract in which a woman talks about men in generic terms.

Extract 17
KO, female, born 1907, lines 296–308

I: so what about your parents, did you look after your parents when they were old?

KO: well (. . .) I looked after my father. he used to love to come to ((place name)) (.) he came for weeks and I mean weeks at a time. he loved being here, I loved having him and he enjoyed – he was a widower by that time. he enjoyed being looked after. he was never any bother. never never. he enjoyed being looked after, he enjoyed his meals. he was ehm – he played ball. he was very good at footy but he never played here. ((unclear)) I used to wonder why he didn't join one of the clubs here because he was very good at it. you think all these things and it's too late

Extract 18
DI, female, born 1946, lines 1,649–57

I should be pulling my hair out if I was but erm probably that I shouldn't judge other people – that's I think for me it's slightly different because erm with men I mean my husband he's still got a good head of hair. he hasn't lost his hair but I know a lot of men when they get – they start at thirty-five I mean my son now he's twenty-six and he'll say oh I hope I'm like dad and I don't lose my hair 'cause I feel I hope I follow my dad you know. I think it would really worry him his hair.

In extract 17, KO describes just about the entire relationship between her and her elderly father in terms of emotions. Apart from one exception, it is narrated through mental clauses referring to KO's father's emotional states. Interestingly, the father's perspective is maintained also when a potential reference to her own emotions is made: *He was never any bother.* Yet it is the father's emotions which are chosen as the medium through which we see the reality.

DI, in extract 18, brings up men's emotional attitude towards physical appearance, and particularly the issue of balding. The story is dramatised by accessing the informant's son's voice. We do not need to take his mother's words for it, we can 'hear' him worry about his hair and the final *it would really worry him his hair* is a summary of what we heard. Note that it is a summary in which the mother decides that the son would not just worry, he would *really* worry. The emotion seems to go beyond superficiality.

A digression upon men's physical appearance and hair is worth making here. Men's hair seems to play a significant role in the public life of modern-day Britain. Politically, there have been comments on such 'events' as Tony Blair's discomfort with his thinning hair, the alleged negative impact of Alistair Darling's and Frank Dobson's beards on their images, and the belief that William Hague's or Iain Duncan Smith's baldness marks them as unsuitable to lead the Conservative Party or become prime minister of the country. Institutions such as the armed forces, paramilitary organisations, voluntary organisations, employers, schools and churches all attempt to control the form in which hair is displayed. Many social groups permit little deviation from what is 'normal' in terms of length, colour and style. Advertisers remind their audiences about products claiming to conceal changes in hair colouring or loss, to prevent hair loss, and to reverse the loss that has already occurred (for a review of social aspects of hair, see Hallpike, 1969; Synnott, 1993). This public concern about politicians' hair seems to be found also in the lives of 'private' men. The UK's Channel 4 documentary dealing with hair loss (broadcast in February 2001 as part of the *Embarrassing Illnesses* series) showed that men (and indeed women) suffering from hair loss constructed it as nothing short of losing a sense of themselves. The documentary featured a number of men speaking in very emotional terms about the fact that they were balding. This concern or at least its awareness, which I have already alluded to here, can be found in the corpus I am analysing.

Next we have an account of a woman who is constructing shared emotional outlook upon life.

Extract 19
PI, female, born 1902, lines 163–74

> I: and how would you compare your lifestyle in mid-life to what – how it was when you were younger?
>
> PI: In what way? How do you mean? (. . .) well we enjoyed things just the same in the evenings we still went to the concerts and theatres of course we loved the theatre. and fortunately my husband loved the ballet so – and I did so we used to go to the ballet. and things like that and we just carried on in life like that. we had a wonderful life really. And then ehm – he decided that he'd had enough of the building so he retired, he finished with that. and then – so I said well you can come and help me in the shop now.

PI positions herself and her husband as sharing a life of loving to do certain things. Their camaraderie is constructed through their emotions. The joint enjoyment of life is coupled with the separate loves of ballet. They are only separate insofar as having the fortune of being married to a kindred spirit, rather than because of some qualitative difference. Despite PI's explicit positioning of herself and her husband in gender roles, it seems that their emotions are on a par. I would also argue that the reference to the husband's having enough of work is also a reference to an emotional attitude. It seems also that such a momentous decision as retirement was taken by PI's husband because of emotions. He had had enough, was fed up with it: this is not a decision based on rational argument, reasoning. This is an emotional decision.

Finally, in extract 20, a woman constructs men generally in terms of emotions.

Extract 20
EB, female, born 1953, lines 1,138–45

> EB: (...) men have more of a problem I think with age than women do. ehm (.) yeah, women have got a problem with age (.) but I've noticed that (.) women my age haven't got a problem because they are single, they do keep themselves (.) nice. as I say, trying to keep themselves nice. ehm (..) they don't think of themselves as (.) old. (.) but I think men have more got a problem with age. I've got a friend who is fifty, and well he is suicidal at the moment I think.

After a prolonged story about joining a dating agency (unquoted here), EB begins her juxtaposition of men's and women's attitudes towards ageing. What's quite fascinating is that, once again, it seems, she is reversing the gender stereotype and claims that while women worry about their physical appearance changing with age, it is men – referred to generically – who worry more. Women seem to have found a way of coping with the problem (by keeping themselves nice, as EB proposes). Men have not and the identification of the problem or at least its potential scale comes with the reference to the informant's friend who suffers so much that he is suicidal. The extremity of such emotions is, interestingly, akin to those attributed to men by BR in extract 1, quoted at the beginning of the chapter. They are also similar in that both women construct men as emotional weaklings, people who are unable to cope with adversity. The macho man, the man from the stereotype, is nowhere to be seen.

Conclusions

In this chapter I began my polemic discussion with the dominant models of masculinity, be they academic or stereotypical, concerning men's alleged inability to feel or express emotions. Masculinity is supposed to be strong, rational, inexpressive. In the discussion above I showed that both men's and women's narratives on experiences of age can (and indeed do) construct both men and masculinity in terms of emotionality, and this emotionality is more often than not 'positive': it is about caring, worrying, loving, enjoying. Emotions can be constructed as part of 'masculine nature' but, on the other hand, they do not have to be. Emotions can be positioned in parallel to masculinity, but not interacting with it.

To say that all this suggests various kinds of masculinity constructs would be trying to re-heat old news; researchers know about this already, even though occasionally they tend to forget to see gender as interacting with age or class, or even ethnicity, or perhaps with illness or disability, or baldness, or single fatherhood, or perhaps with a host of other factors which are relevant within men's life stories, and not necessarily to academics' interests.

Of course I am not claiming to have discovered a new model of masculinity (lived or academic), in one way or another constructed by the interviewed men. I would even venture a guess that, if asked a specific question on masculinity, most of the informants would have tapped into the stereotypes of masculinity expected of them. Men would have probably become 'unemotional'. So I am merely postulating that the stereotypes and models of masculinity are simply too crude to apply to all men, at all times, in all situations. There are times when such models do not work, and I would even hypothesise that they do not work more often than they do. The 'lived' model of masculinity is considerably more complex than the one masculinity literature has us believe, and this is the point I shall be making a number of times in this book.

What I am suggesting here, and will be over the course of this book, is a more radical exploration of masculinities in general and masculinities and emotions in particular. The questions I have in mind are those of the contexts in which emotions may or may not find their ways into masculine narratives and thus contextualise performed masculinity or gender even further and show it as much more context-sensitive than much of the gender research allows for. In the next two chapters, however, I shall change the perspective of my inquiry. This time I shall not be interested in the lived model of masculinity, but I shall explore the strategies used by men when they talk about their emotions.

Appendix: Original Polish version of extract 1

BR: (...) mężczyźni... pierwsi pracę stracili najmniej z ten... a po drugie są takie duże dzieci nie mają charakteru kompletnie załamują się najlepiej

jakby im pozwolono to by się wszyscy powiesili i mieliby z główki dużo
płaczą dużo narzekają a tak mało robią w tym w tym chcą wielki szum
żeby był ale taki... *mało praktyczni* są. nie nie widzę ich może kiedyś jak
były te groty i i i ten i szedł z dzidą i złapał zwierzę no darmo żeby ta
kobieta upolowała, teraz to się tak spłaszczyło że głowa boli a tu takie
życie to jest teraz taka dżungla taka walka o byt oni się nie nadają oni
może by się do dżungli nadali ale tu do tej miejskiej dżungli *absolutnie,
nie!* kobiety są praktyczniejsze i mądrzejsze (.) to mówiłam ja

AZ: [laughter] a jak to wygląda w twojej rodzinie?

BR: to co powiedziałam *jak wyżej dokładnie dokładnie* to samo

Notes

1. The research was carried out in the Institute of Psychology at the University of
   Opole in Poland by Aleksandra Zarosa for her MA dissertation. She interviewed women whose husbands either were unemployed, or earned considerably less than their wives. I am indebted to her for making this extract
   available to me. The quoted extract is my translation of the Polish original
   which can be found in the Appendix above.
2. I put the 'negative' in between inverted commas, as I do not believe that one
   can assign universal value to emotions and label them as positive or negative.
   Such an evaluation must be context-bound. I can imagine contexts (e.g.,
   those of abuse) in which the supposedly negative anger will be positive, as
   well as ones in which the supposedly positive love will, in fact, be negative.

3
'There is a Concern': Strategies of Emotion Talk

Introduction

In this chapter I am beginning to explore the ways in which men speak about their emotions. I am interested in how emotions are constructed in men's narratives of past emotional experiences. Here, as well as in the next chapter, I shall only be interested in men's narratives. The issue of how women talk about men's emotions would merit a different study, as it would offer more insight into women's discursive practices, rather than men's. I shall focus here upon two super-strategies of men's accounts of their emotions: first I shall explore distancing strategies (i.e., strategies in which emotional states are not ascribed directly to those who are constructed as experiencing them); second, I shall be interested in their counterpart: accounts in which men talk about their emotions directly.

By way of a reminder, I take the social constructionist approach to emotions, and view them as experienced via the social and cultural process. The physiological sensations accompanying some emotions are viewed as incidental, and it is discursive practice which is seen as constitutive of emotions and emotional experience. The approach not only views emotions as culture-specific, variable in place and time, but also sees the discursive practices which are used to comment upon and manage individuals' emotional feelings and displays as offering insight into their management, interpretation and representation, the entire 'psychology' of what humans term emotions (Harré and Stearns, 1995). Such emotions as anger, love and hatred are not in one way or another 'housed' inside our bodies or souls, but rather are ways of speaking about how we feel. Emotions have to be 'done', they do not happen automatically (Hearn, 1993). To paraphrase Harré (1991), to be angry or to be in love means to take on an angry or 'in-love' position.

Distancing

One of the most noticeable features of the corpus under consideration here is that in a preponderance of men's accounts emotions are dealt with by means of what could be termed distancing. In their stories male speakers avoided constructing themselves as subjects who had certain feelings or emotions.

I realise that it is difficult to describe a 'canonical' way in which people speak of emotion (see such studies as Lutz, 1990; Haviland and Goldston, 1992; Bamberg 1997a, b; Foolen, 1997; Anderson and Leaper, 1998; Kidron and Kuzar, 2002). Fiehler (2002) proposes that when people describe their emotions (as opposed to expressing them) they may focus on six basic aspects of their experience:

(a) the carrier of the experience;
(b) the type of the experience;
(c) the intensity;
(d) the dynamics;
(e) the object or point of the experience;
(f) the bases of experience and yardsticks of the evaluating statement.

While plausible, it seems to me that the model is unnecessarily broad. Elements (c) and (d) are no more than qualifiers of element (b). Element (f) does not in fact describe the experience itself and thus is different from the rest of the model elements. What we are left with is a three-element linguistic model of emotional experience: the emoter, the emotion and its object.

There are two points that I would like to make with regard to this. The object of an emotion is also an optional element, one which can but does not have to be included in the model. This is not only because of researchers who argue people can experience emotions for no apparent reason (Johnson-Laird and Oatley, 1989) but, more importantly here, because one can imagine contexts in which people deny having an object of their emotions. Someone can easily respond to a question as to why he or she is angry with something like: 'I just am. No particular reason.' Second, I would argue that, linguistically, one needs to break down element (b) of Fiehler's model: his assumption is a relatively homogeneous description of emotion. And still, while one can say 'I love you', one can also say ' I feel love', separating the emotion from 'emoting'.

It is noteworthy that such a proposal seems to be also a reflection of folk, and probably to an extent psychological, theories of emotions which have emotions contained within the body (on metaphorical rendering of emotions, see, e.g., G. Lakoff, 1987; G. Lakoff and Johnson, 1980) and which people in one way or another feel. If emotions are to be felt, it is safe to assume that linguistic constructions of accounts of emotions, if direct, should have direct references to those who feel, the process of feeling, and the emotions themselves (with the latter two elements being occasionally rendered by one verb). Indeed, Kidron and Kuzar (2002) propose that the major cultural script of encoding emotion in English is to place the experiencer in the subject position, with the subject 'controlling' her or his mental situation.

Thus the makeshift model of linguistic expression of emotions could be that *an emoter feels a particular emotion*. A similar approach is favoured by Lutz (1990) who sees 'personalisation' of emotions (i.e., self's ownership of emotions) as a direct way of speaking of emotional experience. And I shall assume that forms deviating from such constructions are used with the function of separating the 'emoter' from the 'emotions'.

Lutz also proposes that personalisation can be seen as a template for generating distancing strategies (i.e., discursive means by which emotions can be distanced from the Self). It seems, however, that Lutz's model is a combination of formal and content categories: she focuses upon the present tense or the presence of negation in the clause and, at the same time, on the 'cause' or 'object' of the emotion. The distancing strategies therefore are about, to use a term discussed by Bavelas and her associates (1990), the dissolution of the 'ownership' of emotion. I realise that Bavelas and her collaborators proposed viewing such linguistic strategies in terms of equivocation, describing it as non-straightforward, ambiguous or obscure (Bavelas *et al.*, 1990:28) but I do not share their views, as I do not think that expressions in which the social actor is not rendered the linguistic one are particularly equivocal or ambiguous. There is no uncertainty of meaning, no 'semantic nebula' in such expressions (Su, 1994), no deception potential (Galasiński, 2000). This is precisely why I also choose the term 'distancing'.

Distancing strategies may of course consist of ambiguous expressions. I follow Su (1994) also in understanding ambiguity, as opposed to equivocation or vagueness. A linguistic item is ambiguous if it satisfies two conditions. Semantically, it must be capable of having two or more distinct meanings (senses or references) but, pragmatically, those meanings must be capable of an interpretation which is tenable in a given context.

Now, Lutz's proposal, probably because it was geared for insight into the cultural notion of controlling emotions, takes account of only one of the elements in the informal model of linguistic encoding of emotional experience, the emoter; and yet distancing strategies can relate to all three of its elements. So, theoretically, distancing expressions can make non-direct references to who feels, and to what in fact he or she does with an emotion, and what it is that he or she feels. It is important to note that the strategies of distancing I propose below are not merely those which are logically implied by the model. The categories I present here are also data-driven in that they were the strategies actually used by the informants. I have identified five strategies of distancing the speaker from the emotion they talked about:

1 The informants constructed situations, events or relationships, rather than the speakers themselves, in terms of emotions.
2 They positioned themselves as objects or targets of emotional states caused by such events.
3 They constructed emotions as experienced by unspecified emoters.
4 They showed emotions as objects.
5 They constructed themselves, their relationships or situations in terms which did not specify the emotions underpinning them.

The first three strategies rely on making a non-direct or ambiguous reference to who actually is the 'holder' of emotional states referred to; the emoter is not positioned as a senser in an actor's position in the linguistic expression. The first two do it by positioning the emotions as external to human subjects, while the third strategy makes an ambiguous reference to the emoter. The fourth strategy makes a non-direct reference to what the emoter's relationship with an emotion is. Thus emoters will not 'feel' emotions, but rather will have them, get them or whatever. The fifth strategy makes an ambiguous reference to what kind of emotions a person has. However, depending on the depth of implication, the strategy can also consist of making non-direct or ambiguous references to all three elements of the model. Needless to say, the above strategies are not mutually exclusive and more often than not are used by speakers in one utterance, or even jointly in one account of emotion. Furthermore, one linguistic expression can employ a number of distancing strategies at the same time. In what follows, for reason of clarity, I shall discuss them separately.

Emotion-events

As has just been noted, one of the strategies of speakers' distancing from their emotional states consists in constructing events in terms of experienced emotions. Speakers chose to speak of 'happy occasions', 'happy married lives', as well as 'periods of intense anxiety'. Instead of describing themselves as happy in their marriages, or being anxious for the spouse's health, our informants chose to represent those feelings as characteristics of events, or periods of time. Similarly, the informants chose to speak of close or loving relationships, rather than of themselves as actors in those relationships.

Consider the following examples.

Extract 1
WC, male, born 1926, lines 192–204

> WC: but I probably enjoyed my middle years as much as I've enjoyed anything. I mean my – my – if you think about it – from what I've just told you – eh (.) my childhood (.) was very happy. and then came the war years and being in the conflict and coming out with this dreadful thing as well (tuberculosis). you know, that was a terrible part of my life. and just after the war was a terrible part of my life. ehm (.) it's a part I don't really like to dwell on, at all. and then – (.) from when I got married I went on under my own steam so to say my life changed enormously. it changed (for the better) and you know, they were very very good years, all of them. you know, apart from the (blips) and that ((unclear)) but. overall they were very good years.

Extract 2
UT, male, born 1915, lines 776–85

> I: so what do you mean by it became a bit of a bore – what do you mean by –

> UT: erm. because I hadn't erm I hadn't been able to settle down to the fact that I couldn't go to work I couldn't do this I couldn't do that. I couldn't do anything. (.) I was restricted as I say with my complaint – with my arthritis and what have you. and erm it became very tedious. but I never thought about committing suicide like a good many other people.

WC, in extract 1, juxtaposes consecutive periods of his life, starting from his childhood. His narrative changes from a direct form to referring to his emotions via distancing strategies. He begins by a direct reference to his enjoyment of his middle years and this is the only time in the narrative that he speaks of emotions directly. Then, instead of his own experience, he chooses to describe childhood, the war years and adulthood in terms of emotions. Interestingly, only WC's childhood is constructed with an explicit 'emotion label' *happy*. The other two periods are described in terms implying emotions, the war years as 'terrible' and the adult years as 'very very good'.

Although I shall attempt to make some general remarks with reference to distancing strategies, I would like to argue that distancing here might be to do with the implied strength of the emotions. The stronger the emotions, the less likely they are to be referred to directly. And if one were to construct a scale of strength of emotions, enjoyment would score considerably lower than happiness. And so, rather than speaking of being happy, WC chooses to describe his childhood in terms of happiness. Also the war period and the one immediately after are implied to be associated with extreme emotions. They are strong enough for the interviewee not to want to talk about them. Strong emotions are also associated with the subsequent, good period of life. All these emotions are distanced. Such an interpretation could in fact be reinforced by extract 2. UT implies experiences of an extreme nature: ones that led others to suicidal thoughts. But the informant choses not to refer to what he felt; instead he chooses a very understated way of referring to his experience: *it became very tedious*. Arguably, as in the previous extract, it is the strength of the emotional experience that contributed to the speaker's choice to distance himself from his emotions.

One could speculate therefore that in negotiating their narratives and their expressions of emotions, the informants chose to speak directly about emotions which are tame, not extreme. Perhaps negotiating their subject positions (with masculinities possibly imposed by the context of the interview) in the local context of the interview, they decided that it would be unseemly for a man to speak of extreme emotions, be it 'negative' (unhappiness) or 'positive' (happiness). Perhaps the former implies too much of a weakness, the other too much irrationality. This speculation is in line with the cultural models of emotion which I mentioned in Chapter 1. Emotions are seen in terms of uncontrollability or danger. One can only add that the stronger the emotion, the more uncontrollable it would seem to be. But at the same time, one could also use the local face constraints (see Goffman, 1959, and Brown and Levinson, 1987, for a discussion of face) in accounting for the distancing strategies. After all, it is probably quite difficult to speak about strong emotions to a complete stranger, such as the interviewer, and especially if one speaks about such emotions as unhappiness. There is of course no need to assume that it must be one explanation or the other; it might well be a combination of the two.

The distancing strategies in the next two examples serve not only to make a non-direct reference to the emoter, but also imply that that the man speaking is not the only one whose emotions are talked about.

Extract 3
IF, male, born 1947, lines 386–93

> I: and can you describe what it was like when your daughter moved out?
>
> IF: well (.) permanently (.) it sort of crept up on us. I mean the night we left her at university (.) she didn't go in halls, she went into a students' house. and that night was pretty traumatic, the drive back down the M6 was pretty dramatic. (.) so we've been used to her not being here. (. . .)

Extract 4
CL, male, born 1922, lines 77–90

> I: mmh. (.) how would you say learning this affected your lifestyle? did your life change after she was diagnosed?
>
> CL: well it was more – it was more restricted. ehm she went through quite long periods of remission. so we could go on – eh well we – we didn't take foreign holidays for instance, because we never felt sufficiently confident to do that. but there were eh – we just led a normal, as I say, day-to-day life. (.) and ehm (.) there were short periods when she had to go into hospital for an operation, I mean those were periods of intense anxiety. but then it righted itself and (.) that's how we went on. so that was a decade, I suppose that covers late middle age doesn't ((laughs)) to to sixty-one.

In extract 3, the trauma and drama of the situation is rendered merely as a facet of the event, rather than agentivised in terms of those who actually did have the clearly implied emotions. The speaker's narrative changes from the agentive rendering of the 'leaving' of the informant's daughter (we have no doubt as to *who* left the daughter at the university), to the agent-free representation of driving home, by virtue of 'the drive'. The nominalisation (a linguistic process of rendering actions or processes as objects) not only changes the action into an event, but also helps detach the clearly implied feelings on the part of the informant and his wife from them and ascribe them to the event itself. While it is acceptable to do the leaving, it seems less acceptable to do the emoting. Extract 4 is similar not only in the use of nominalisations, but also in the implication that the emotions which are referred to (such as anxiety) are shared between the speaker and his wife. Once again, as I showed in the previous chapter, emotions cross the gender lines in the narratives under analysis.

Targets of emotions

Detachment of emotional states from the self was also achieved by the speakers positioning themselves as objects or targets of emotional states which are a result of something external to the feeling subjects. Here, on the one hand, speakers chose to describe things as worrying them and, on the other, explicitly spoke of events as sources of emotions, directly positioning them as external to themselves. In this way speakers spoke of 'suffering from very great insecurity' (note the invocation of medical connotation in such a formulation) or chose to describe one's children as a 'source of great joy'. The emotions in such constructions are also positioned as being at least generated outside the feeling subjects who are their targets. Witness the following two examples.

Extract 5
SE, male, born 1951, lines 555–72

I: So would you say that you are looking after your father now?

SE: No. no he's – he's still well able to look after himself. if anything he's ehm, he's looking after my sister which is a slight source of ((unclear)).

I: A slight source of what?

SE: ((unclear)) ehm well annoying. ehm 'cus I don't think he should have to but that's another story. so as far as he's concerned now he's still self-sufficient although obviously as he's getting older he's getting a little less capable than he was. he was – he was a big guy I mean he was forever digging and growing and what have you. He's less able to do that now so I just (.) I suppose him by persuading that he doesn't actually have to do that anymore ((slight laugh)).

Extract 6
NI, male, born 1953, lines 793–818

I: Ehm what do you associate with people being in their prime?

NI: (. . .) ((long pause)). I think middle age is in your prime if you're fit. I think it really is the best time of your life really. yeah. I think from – from early thirties to about now. I think I've definitely been in my prime.

healthier, fitter, no drugs in my systems, know what's going on around me. yeah. clearer thinking. less worries really. less insecurities in some ways. feel more – when you're in your thirties you're more confident, you know what's going on. you – you shouldn't worry about too many things.

I: Is there anything you are at the age ((unclear))

NI: I don't know that why it's – they're such awkward questions you're asking me 'cus (. . .) technically I'm thinking I'm nearly fifty but in myself I'm thinking I still feel alright. but it's that worrying number fifty that's creeping up on me. and I can actually see – I am – I am starting to look a bit – a bit wrinkly. I'm seeing I look a bit old and yeah. It doesn't last long, I don't dwell on it, it doesn't upset me it just. I suppose it's creeping up slowly, just. (. . .) I think stopping smoking has probably given me another lease of life yeah.

Extract 5 contains probably the most explicit construction of a situation as a cause or source of the speaker's emotions. The speaker's annoyance with the situation of his elderly father having to look after his daughter does not originate within the speaker but, rather, outside him. This is quite a safe way of constructing emotions which are likely to be perceived as negative. One should not, probably, be annoyed with one's father or sister. By distancing himself in the way he is, the speaker relieves himself of the responsibility for being annoyed. It is the situation that is annoying. He is merely the object.

In extract 6, on the other hand, NI uses a number of distancing strategies apart from the one I am discussing now. His references to 'less worries' indicates that he is taking emotions as objects; by using the impersonal 'you', he ambiguates the emoter. But what is particularly interesting here is his reference to the 'worrying number fifty' and the parallelism of the linguistic form after the reference to emotions. The speaker not only constructs himself as the object of the worrying state of being 50 years old, but, immediately after that, he constructs it as 'creeping up' on him. The parallelism seems to reinforce the construction of 'being worried' rather than worrying. Moreover, the speaker constructs the age of 50 not merely as worrying only him. The expression 'worrying number fifty' indicates the universality of the age's characteristic. It is not only NI who might be worried; this is a more universal matter.

The last example I shall discuss here is also interesting because of the shift from a distancing strategy to speaking directly of the speaker's emotions.

Extract 7
CG, male, born 1930, lines 285–92

> I: right – what would you say then when did you first become aware of your own mortality?
>
> CG: I suppose at the death of my father. That's the first time I began to think of it. Curiously it has worried me less than I suspect it worries most people. (.) Because I'm an atheist so I don't fear anything is going to happen to me after death. Just afraid of the dying.

As I will suggest in more general terms later, the shift from distancing is to do with the shift from the informant's speaking of his relationships with others as opposed to emotions directed at himself. He begins by speaking of his emotions in terms of a relationship with his father and this is how his father's death is constructed, as something that has had an impact upon him. The emotions he speaks of are introduced in a distancing strategy: death and mortality are to do with relationships and, just like his father left him, he is going to leave his family. The moment, however, moves on to his atheist stance, when the emotions become directly referenced. His emotions are purely his own concern, there are no relationships involved. In the same way, he is afraid of dying: facing death, once again he speaks of his emotions directly. The three references to emotions – one with the use of distancing strategy (worrying) and the two direct ones (fearing, and being afraid) – place emotion in the same area of emotional experience which Wierzbicka (1999:72) denotes with 'bad things can happen'. Despite that, CG chooses a different strategy to describe his emotions in different contexts. In other words, it is not the linguistic form (particularly the common 'worry' used with human patients) that controls what is being said, but it is chosen to suit the strategy.

More generally, conventional expressions such as 'I was pleased', 'I was devastated' or 'I was concerned', because of appearing in the passive voice might be taken as akin to the strategy I have now discussed. I don't think it is the case, because there is no active voice equivalent that speakers could avail themselves of. The speakers cannot put themselves as linguistic actors in expressing such emotions, and thus I would take such expressions as expressing emotions directly. This is in contrast to such expressions as 'I was worried' or 'Things worry me', which do have an active voice equivalent in 'I worry'. Thus they can be taken as a distancing strategy.

Unspecified emoters

The final strategy focusing on the emoter consists in the ambiguation of who it is that has the feelings referred to. The three examples I am going to present here refer to different ways in which speakers employed the strategy.

Extract 8
ST, male, born 1950, lines 400–14

> I: how do you feel about your children growing up and leaving home?
>
> ST: I wouldn't say we can't wait although sometimes you think you can't wait (.) I mean – you do notice them getting bigger and older and in fact it's been very noticeable for the past year I suppose in how keen they are in taking more control over their own lives which sometimes means making more demands on ours. (.) it's about time that they went – well that John went. he's old enough now. he needs to break away. I mean he was away last term. he was missed and then he came back and he's been back since. it's been very strange. you get used to them being away. and then they come back and its permanent not – not just for a vacation.

Extract 9
BH, born 1940, lines 414–27

> I: mmh. ehm can you describe to me how it was when your other children left home?
>
> (.)
>
> BH: great! ((loud laugh)) no ehm (.) you – I think you always worry about them, initially. again, as time goes by you get less worried about them. they seem quite happy and content in what they do, where they go like ((daughter)) went to ((town)) and that way, ((other daughter)) went up to ((town)) and then to (.) we were concerned about them at first. especially ((other daughter)) being so far (.) away. ehm but again as time goes by they seem to be able to look after themselves, so (.) we don't worry about it now.

While in extract 8 the distancing is carried out by the deletion of the emoting agent rendered by the passive voice, in extract 9 the speaker chooses to change the perspective to a generic principle of worrying about one's children. Both informants, apart from avoiding positioning themselves as either missing or worrying about their children, also leave the implication of their spouses sharing these emotions. The implication is weaker in extract 8, where the speaker begins by introducing the 'we' perspective. In extract 9, the perspective of the two spouses is introduced after the distancing strategy, and also when ascribing emotions to both parents. What the speaker does, I think, is position fatherhood and motherhood on a par. Fathers and mothers worry in the same way. The gender line is crossed again.

In contrast to the previous extracts, in the following one the speaker does not change the subject position. What he says leaves little doubt that his distancing strategy is about his own emotions.

Extract 10
SE, male, born 1951, lines 633–44

I: ehm when you got separated was that something that made you think about your age in – in the sense of were you thinking that you would get married again?

SE: (..) the reason for getting married is – was nothing to do with age. I think that would've been whatever age. it – it wasn't about age it was about (.) well obviously (.) falling in love with somebody ehm it's about ehm friendship and companionship etc. and wanting to ehm (.) put a seal on that. so. making this commitment, that's why I married, that's nothing to do with age 'cus age is irrelevant as far as that's concerned.

If we start with the end of the turn, we can see that the speaker was in fact speaking about his own marriage and the reasons why he got married. One of these reasons seems to be falling in love. However, the moment we look at the turn from its beginning, the obviousness of what I have said disappears. One could easily interpret the informant's words as an account of a potential situation, a general principle. This generalisation is at its peak in the utterance precisely when SE is talking about his falling in love. There is no explicit reference to the loving agent, to whoever did fall in love, even in generic terms. And yet the speaker switches the perspective to himself when he stops talking about emotions (love, friendship, companionship, even the wish to 'put a seal'). The only clue as to the emoting agent might be the verb *was* right at the beginning of the turn, which suggests that the act of getting married did in fact happen. Still the clue disappears, if you like, the moment the speaker moves to talking about emotions; the verb vanishes and there is no indication as to whether the falling in love did in fact happen, let alone who was the person in love. The reference to love contains also the backgrounding of the target of the emotion: the speaker talks about 'somebody' rather than his wife. Also 'friendship' and 'companionship', clearly associated with emotions (if not in fact also labels of emotions), have not only no emoter, but also no target of the emotions, presumably reciprocating them. The distancing is just about complete; there is no hint that it is in fact the speaker himself who has fallen in love and feels empathy toward his wife. It could be argued that such constructions are also similar to the next strategy I shall discuss, that of positioning emotions as objects. In addition, SE positions his love and other emotions as 'out there' to be acknowledged, rather than experienced. The speaker very carefully removes any reference to his own emotions, indirectly identifying them only after he has finished talking about them.

Emotion-objects

Distancing from one's emotional experiences is also done by constructing the emotions as things existing in the world independently of anyone who might experience them. Linguistically, this strategy consists of non-direct reference to the emoter's relationship with an emotion. Thus emoters will not 'feel' emotions but, rather, have them, get them and so on. The strategy is aimed at changing the mental process (feeling) normally associated with representations of emotions to material, relational or existential processes which situate the actor clauses referring to 'doing' (taking a dislike), 'having' (having worries) or 'being' (there being concerns) (on process, see Halliday and Hasan, 1985; Halliday, 1994). Thus the strategy, while acknowledging the 'holder' of the emotion, does not position it in terms of its 'experiential' value: see the following extracts.

Extract 11
ST, male, born 1950, lines 446–54

I: how has your relationship with your parents been developing as you get older?

ST: (. .) well my mother is a bit of a concern now because she's had a stroke. (.) so (.) there's a slight worry about her all the time (.) but I suspect I grew away from her quite early on. so although there's concern it's – don't have a great deal of contact. usually telephone about once a week or something.

Extract 12
DQ, male, born 1957, lines 735–46

> I: ehm ehm, so that generally would you say that these kinds of relation-
> ships have become more or less important to you or has it been (.) the
> same?
>
> DQ: it's – it's – it's just that – it must have become less important because
> I've not done anything about it myself and not – not – not really interested.
> Our ehm (..) we – other than this one aunt that – that I have particular
> fondness for that we lost before Christmas ehm (.) the ehm contacts with
> the family are very very few (.) and are generally through my parents who –
> who in actual fact ehm I've noticed in recent years are actually making
> more effort to keep in contact.

In both cases the informants speak of their emotions towards others
in a distanced way. While DQ in extract 12 constructs his emotions in
terms of 'having', ST, in extract 11, goes much further in his attempt to
construct an object. The existential clause (constituted by the copula *is*)
indicates the existence of an emotion somewhere out there, so to speak.
Also the emoter is backgrounded in this case. But the informant's
distancing comes in another form as well in that the person who is
defined in terms of an emotion, the informant's mother, *is bit of a
concern*. This objectification of the emotion also serves the function of
ambiguating the person who might be concerned.

In the next extract the speaker seems to juggle a distancing strategy
and a direct reference to himself.

Extract 13
NI, male, born 1953, lines 455–74

> I: What did you get impatient about?
>
> NI: Just what they were doing and where they were going. and I wasn't
> interested. they didn't change. they continued to do the same things that
> they'd always done. sounds like me really ((slight laugh)). ((unclear)) it's
> only people I used to know that I was brought up with, hung around with
> all through my late twenties and early thirties. they seemed to stay in that –
> in that period of time and they didn't move on. it's like you've probably
> heard about these sixties nights and seventies nights and they go to
> places like that. and I'm not sure psychologically whether it's my fear of
> being stuck in that age or whether I am generally not interested. I'm
> looking – I'm always looking forward and what's happening now. so I still
> get – a lot of people get stuck in the culture of their youth and stay in

that time period. that horrifies me a bit. it's some sort of entrapment that I don't want to know about. and they play the music that they used to play when they were in their twenties and whatever.

In his disapproval of his milieu, the informant talks about the reason why he wanted to move on. Wondering whether it was his 'fear' or whether he was 'not interested', he switches between a distancing strategy and a direct reference to himself. He seems to make a choice of not referring to being afraid in direct terms, and referring directly to being interested. It is even more noteworthy if one sees the reference to fear in a slightly larger context. In terms of personal reference, the story first weaves between references to 'they' and to 'I', only to settle the focus upon 'I'. The only break in this pattern is precisely the reference to the speaker's fear which is rendered by the possessive pronoun 'my'. Only the reference to an emotional state is not positioning the speaker as active, taking life in his own hands.

I do not think that there is a good explanation for such a marked shift in the narrative without recourse to the stereotype of unemotional man. Emotions seem to be unwanted by the speaker: they are an unwelcome part of his story. Still, they are part of it and, presumably driven by the truth bias (the tendency to tell the truth), the speaker tells the interviewer about them, especially that the question did concern emotions. So he does it in a distanced and, at the same time, safer way, potentially less threatening to his masculinity, both locally (in the local context of speaking to the interviewer, a younger woman) and more globally, satisfying the stereotype.

Unspecified emotions

The last strategy of distancing the speaker from his emotions involves making an ambiguous reference to what kind of emotions a person has. However, the strategy is particularly likely to be used for ambiguating other elements of the 'emotion model'. In the corpus, the most frequent use of this strategy was in reference to the kind of relationships informants were in. In other words, instead of talking about the kind emotions informants had for someone (e.g., wife, child or parent), and vice versa, they chose to describe relationships in terms which implied such emotions.

In the three extracts I am going to analyse here, the speakers use different ways in which to imply their emotions by talking about their relationships. In extract 14, we witness quite a complicated account of relationships between the informant and his parents.

Extract 14
SE, male, born 1951, lines 538–53

> I: How has your relationship with your parents been developing during your forties?
>
> SE: OK well my (. .) my mother I was always very close to and before she died early in the period. ehm (.) of lung cancer. my father (.) it was always a little more aloof. I always had a slightly more – it was not difficult relationship with him but it just (.) not formal, I don't think he interacts well and so I disrespected that and ehm didn't ehm – you know. we were close but not – not perhaps as close as I was with my mother. when my mother died obviously I think he needed a little more than we had before and we developed that quite well so we keep in close touch. (.) talk to him at least weekly, visit regularly and ehm make sure that he's ok and ehm keep the lines of communication up.

In extract 14, SE begins with a direct ascription of an attribute to himself ('I was close') when he talks about his mother. When he moves to talk about the relationship with his father, he chooses the 'we' perspective, something he never does in respect to his mother. Despite the use of 'we' in reference to more distance between him and his father, SE changes the perspective to himself again when he refers to his closeness to his mother in their relationship which he never constructs in terms of reciprocation. In contrast, the relationship with his father is narrated in quite a complicated way. The ragged narrative, with plenty of halts and repairs, suggests perhaps some difficulty in making the account. The informant distances himself from the implied emotions even further. SE chooses to use the pronoun 'it' which is identified only a bit later as referring to his relationship with his father. The relationship becomes an entity in its own right, with the people involved deleted from the linguistic form. In such a way, it is not merely the emotions which are unspecified or unclear: there is no one to feel them. But then the speaker offers an explanation for the kind of relationship he has with his father and decides that his father has difficulty interacting with people. And it is only after telling us about his disrespect for this that he decides to characterise the relationship in terms of a certain closeness, almost as an afterthought.

What is striking in SE's account of the relationship with his father is the joint contribution to it by himself and his father, or, should I say the shared responsibility for the lack of closeness. Thus we hear that the father had difficulty interacting and that the informant disrespected it, a parallel construction of two men who do not contribute positively to a relationship. A consequence of this is the subsequent 'we' perspective. This 'joint contribution' to a relationship can also be seen in the narrative in extract 15.

Extract 15
IF, male, born 1947, lines 429–54

> I: how has your relationship with your parents developed as you have been getting older?
>
> IF: better. (.) I mean my childhood years: fine. eh (.) but from when I started work (.) I'm being honest (.) until I started courting ((wife)) when I was twenty-two (.) me and my dad didn't get on. (.) no (.) I couldn't do it right. (.) he was always (.) I was either out too late or – I could do nothing right. ehm I mean it was the sixties, I had a motor-scooter, I was a mod, yeah, I had my parka, with the fur put on and the flags (.) the lights on and the wing mirrors. yeah. never I got into no trouble. but I couldn't – no, me dad and me didn't see eye to eye. dad never had an interest in sport (.) it was his garden, as it still is now. (.) but as soon as I started courting with ((wife)), and we settled down (.) it changed. and we're the best of friends now. (.) I mean I've got a different relationship with ((son)). (.) we do things together. dad never did. (.) and I think that's the difference between my mid-life and Dad's. dad had a push-bike to go to work and come back from work. spent a lot of time at work. but didn't involve himself in much with what was going on within the family and leisure. (.) I only remember him taking me to the pictures a couple of times. things like that. (.) but there's more going on now. (.) there's a lot more going on, there's a lot more for people to now than what there was (.) back then.

This time, the distancing from the speaker's emotions is carried by means of a reference to a relationship which is rendered in much more active terms. Not getting on is seconded by not being able to see eye to eye. Although the relationship is very much described as contributed to equally by both father and son ('me and my dad'), we can of course see that the overall responsibility for it is put on the father. Still, this construction of the 'equal contribution' also has the consequence of implying 'joint' emotions. It is not only his own emotions that speaker does not wish to make explicitly manifest. Needless to say, these emotions are never specified. I think this distancing strategy must also be viewed in terms of providing speakers with a 'shortcut' to their emotions. The relationships of parents (especially the so-called difficult relationships), with children involve a host of emotions and it is not easy to define such emotions in simple terms. This strategy offers a way out of the problem. You don't have to talk about what you feel; you can talk about what kind of relationship you have and imply the feelings.

There is a problem with such an argument, though, especially in this particular instance in which the interviewer asks an explicit question about the interviewee's relationships. Just as Sigmund Freud is reputed to have said 'A cigar is sometimes just a cigar', one could also say that speaking of relationships is sometimes just speaking of relationships and serves precisely that purpose; the postulate of distancing might be somewhat overdone. But then the interviewee could very well respond to such a question by saying: 'We love each other.' And in fact the informant does not respond with a 'grammatical match' to the interviewer's question. I do not think there is a way out of such a problem. People can speak of their relationships just for that purpose. On the other hand, as I postulate here, they can speak of their relationships in order to distance themselves from their emotions, in order to avoid speaking directly about what they feel. The decision as to which one is the right interpretation is nigh impossible to make, perhaps because the communicative intentions and goals of the speakers are not available for empirical scrutiny. Speakers' self-reflection is definitely not a fool-proof method. What we are left with therefore is a degree of uncertainty which could only be reduced, for example, by more and more thorough insight into larger discursive context, but probably never removed. I would suggest that such a difficulty might not be as acute in the next extract.

Extract 16
DQ, male, born 1957, lines 615–28

I: But you said you're also kind of looking for them [children] to get independent?

DQ: Yeah, it's the nurturing process and making sure that they are fit – they have those skills – survival skills, they have the common sense of – they have that ((unclear)) to be able go forth and live on their own and do what they want to do and instil that confidence and self-esteem that they can do and that's what I – what I really want. Yes, they are important to me, they always will be (.) ehm but (.) the importance at the moment is making sure that they are getting the best overall education not only at school but in everything else that they are getting a life education as well (.) that is really important to me.

The speaker here chooses yet another way of implementing the distancing strategy: he chooses an attribute to predicate of his children. Out of quite a number of possibilities of describing his emotions towards and relationship with his children, he chooses to call them important. It seems also that here the strategy might serve as a shortcut in expressing a host of emotions. But, at the same time, such a construction is quite good at hiding any emotions the speaker might have.

Here we cross the boundary between what Su (1994) calls ambiguity (which I described earlier) and vagueness. Vagueness introduces the presence of uncertainty of meaning; it is – as Su (1994:116) puts it – a semantic nebula. Pragmatically, vagueness can be described in terms of uncertainty in deciding the applicability of meaning. Both phenomena seem to be capable of deception as both can render the speaker as being *not* accountable for any meaning inferred (see Bradac, Friedman and Giles, 1986). Of course I am not suggesting that the informant is trying to deceive. It would be quite implausible to assume here that in an utterance full of care, one particular element is in fact deceptive. What I am proposing, rather, is that the strategy as used by DQ could in fact be used as a means not only of distancing a speaker from his or her emotions, but also implying those he or she might not in fact have. Thinking children important suggests strongly positive emotions towards them; however, such a suggestion might be quite misleading.

Even though the strategy of not specifying emotions, implying them, rather than making them explicit, mostly occurs when speakers talk about their relationships, it is by no means the only use to which it is put. Consider the following example.

Extract 17
WC, male, born 1926, lines 346–56

I: mmh can you remember what it was like when your children left home?

WC: ((clears throat)) very quiet, very quiet. yes we – it was eh (.) eh (.) it was like living in a mausoleum. although – they both lived in the same area. and so we saw them quite a lot so that sort of softened the blow ((unclear)). and of course there were compensations as well. because when they were teenagers and they were out late eh (.) nobody went to sleep until they were in and things like that (certainly).

The beginning of this account of the children's home-leaving is quite dramatic. We can almost hear the museum-like silence the speaker tells about. This is the set for speaking about the blow of the new situation. The informant implies very strong emotions on his and his wife's part. The reference to the compensations of living on their own is in fact an interesting reinforcement to implying the strong emotions behind the blow. It is juxtaposed with the practice of staying up late waiting for the adolescent children to come home safely at night. Only those who care, who love, would do any such thing.

Feeling men

The examples quoted up until now seem to square well both with the stereotypical views of masculinity and with its academic models. In fact, above I suggested in reference to some of the instances of distancing that it would be difficult to explain them without referring to the stereotype of the unemotional man. But, as I argued in Chapter 1, the fact that men avail themselves of discursive strategies which might be associated with a certain stereotype or ideologies of masculinity does not constitute masculinity or any traits in them. Men perform masculinities in contexts which are imbued with gender politics, concerns of face and countless other factors, and some choose to use distancing strategies in such contexts. This is the theoretical point. The extrapolation of such narratives as those I have just analysed on an unemotional masculinity does not make sense empirically. Alongside the distancing strategies, there were narratives with direct references to emotions. In those narratives men spoke directly of their worries, their anger, their happiness, their fear. There is very little doubt that men are not only capable of expressing their emotions, but that they in fact do put that capacity to ample use. In what follows, I shall show three extended extracts in which the informants speak directly of a number of their emotions.

The extracts given are only a small part of the corpus of narratives in which men spoke directly of their emotions. Because of their relative linguistic uniformity – there is just about only one way in which one can speak directly of emotions – there is little point in discussing more examples. Linguistically, the direct references are considerably less interesting than distancing strategies. Moreover, what I shall discuss provides plenty of evidence to counter those models which construct men as in one way or another out of touch with their emotions, incapable of expressing or speaking about them. The burden of proof for my claim that such blanket models are implausible seems to lie in showing an instance of a man talking about his emotions. There were of course considerably more instances of explicit references to emotions made by the male informants.

Let me first return to the extract which I have already touched upon in the previous chapter, arguing that the informant positions his explicitly invoked masculinity in parallel to his emotions. Here I would like to focus upon the way he speaks of his emotions, present and past.

Extract 18
KI, male, born 1933, lines 523–65

I: didn't you feel lonely when you were suddenly on your own again?

(.)

KI: not really. (.) not really because I've always had lots of friends. and I mean you don't – these change evolve slowly. so you don't say oh eighteen you don't say ((whistles)) ps! she's gone! that's it. I got nothing on. I mean from say sixteen (.) well (..) ehm I didn't – (.) I didn't have the problems of ensuring that she got the right clothes, for instance. and my son hadn't got the right clothes. it's really very difficult for a man to start thinking of children's clothes. and all the things that children want. and (..) and all the funny things that happen to girls. at times. and (.) and (.) I have (.) I have a memory of my daughter and uff I feel so bad about it now. I didn't really understand at the time and I – I don't know whether she thinks about it. I don't know whether she is – ah I came home (.) I tell you I'm getting very personal there (.) came home one night and (.) she was in bed. and – well she went to bed. and when I went up to see her, she was in tears, crying. and (.) I was furious for some reason or other. I was absolutely fuming, lost my temper with her. I said what's the matter with you? what you're crying for? and ((slight laugh)) she'd – she'd just started her periods and she didn't really, you know – and I was absolutely (.) jumping. because I said come on then – basically ((unclear)) every woman in the world has these, you know, what the hell are you crying for! well over the years various girls have said to me it's a (.) ehm it's a time in a girl's life that is quite ((unclear)) and I (.) regret that time, or that moment very very very much. I really really do. because it wasn't until you know you start talking to people. that some girls find this – well being a man I don't know about these things. and eh ((laughs)) having to go round the chemist's for her on occasions and just. (.) it's just one of these things, so how a woman gets on. a woman – I think with a woman – I think for a start you don't have that problem with a boy. so to some extent, to some extent, a woman left on her own with children is far able to cope more easily than a man is. I couldn't do that again. I could never ever do that again.

KI tells a story of his emotions within and towards a particular event in his single fatherhood. It is not only a story of anger, or fury, as the interviewee puts it, but also a story of his regret for what happened. The informant realises the significance of what happened. He is not only clearly aware of his emotional outburst, but also of the impact upon what happened. He in fact wonders whether his daughter still remembers the situation, or knows that he himself still has an emotional attitude towards it.

The interviewee has no problems with speaking of his emotions. KI's difficulties in the story, highlighted by *uff, I feel so bad about it*, with the paralinguistic *uff* reinforcing the difficulty, is not so much trouble with expressing the emotions, but with coping with what happened, underscored also by his awareness that he is talking about very personal aspects of his and his daughter's lives. The clause explicitly ascribing emotions to the speaker could in fact be seen as facilitating the story which is told in a very dramatic way. The explicit reference to his present emotions is the beginning of the frame introducing the actual story. The frame finishes with a paralinguistically emotional reference to the personal nature of the subject matter.

KI's account of his fury is played out by invoking his voice talking to his daughter. The speaker gives the interviewer a 'witness account', a playback of what happened, as if for the audience to make up their own minds about what happened. So we not only get to hear what the informant said to his daughter, but we are also told about her emotional distress. Still, KI is quite careful to note that his anger was not directed, at least initially, at his daughter. Her difficulty in coping with the onset of menstruation was only a trigger for the release of the accumulated fury. But there is no attempt to justify that. Rather, KI constructs himself as coming to understand what his daughter went through and regretting what happened, and the reference to understanding and regret is the frame closing the story. His present emotions frame his story on both sides. KI appears to be at pains to show his awareness of what happened and his present negative attitude towards it. The explicit declaration of regret is followed by a story explaining how the regret and the understanding of what happened came about. It is told as a story of true (in the sense of the speaker's lived experience) contrition, rather than just a stated one. KI seems to suspect that he might not be believed and thus starts this part of his account with the reinforcement of his statement ('I really really do'), only to support it with an account of his coming to understand what happened. His regret is underpinned not only by understanding of what happened, but also by its later enactment in that KI helps his daughter by going to the chemist's for her.

Now consider the following.

Extract 19
TE, male, born 1950, lines 224–37

> I: So you – you say you don't think about what you're doing in terms of how far you've got in relation to your age. do you feel that other people might look at it that way? (. .) I don't know if your parents or friends or?
>
> TE: Possibly I don't know. it's ehm. It's never bothered me what other people think it's ehm (. .) me. I mean if I'm happy then I'm happy I mean (. .) ((unclear)) pushing me but I don't think mothers would ever be happy whatever you know [. . .] ehm but if you're happy then that's what it comes up to at the end of the day if you're happy doing what you are. ehm (. .) if you're not then it's up to you to change it ehm I don't think there's a – (.) an age thing it's ehm a personal one.

lines 452–61

> I: Ehm what would you say are the most important things to you in your current phase of life?
>
> TE: (. . .) Enjoying yourself. I think if you don't enjoy it I mean that's – you can't force yourself. I mean it – I don't mean you mustn't work at anything 'cus you've got the satisfaction of doing things. it does take work which ehm (. .). yeah yeah – I just – enjoy yourself be true to yourself. ehm (. . .). do what I enjoy yeah. ehm (. . .). yeah that's it really yeah ((slight laugh)).

lines 588–98

> I: Have you ever though about getting married again or you know living with somebody again?
>
> TE: Well no 'cus ehm. I think it comes down to – I'm a loner and always have been. the only time – I'm quite happy with my own company you know. ehm (.) I could talk to myself for ages and not get bored. ehm. no I – I – I – I'm ehm a loner. ehm I – I've had a friend who – who – was moving house and said well come and stay here and we got on each other's nerves and we haven't spoken since ((slight laugh)).

TE tells his stories of happiness, talking about his potential emotions and actual ones. The first fragment shows the unconditionality of his happiness. Moreover, this formula (*if I'm happy then I'm happy*) seems to be a general recipe for happiness. Happiness seems to be a matter of decision, one that he is prepared to take. But it is not to say that this happiness is rational; rather, anyone could decide to be happy! This manifesto of happiness continues in the second fragment in which his *modus vivendi* seems to be focused upon achieving 'positive' emotions. And in the last fragment we have the final chapter of the happy man's story, of someone who seems at peace with himself. He is happy and has no problem with expressing it. The opposite emotions are expressed by the speaker in the next three fragments.

Extract 20
NI, male, born 1953, lines 352–75

> I: Do you ever experience anything resembling some sort of mid-life crisis?
>
> NI: No I can't think. I've been accused of this every I'm having a mid-life crisis.
>
> I: Who is accusing you of that?
>
> NI: I think probably now actually. it's probably this year I'm getting a bit nervous and it's probably brought on by having a new child. I'm thinking aagh, I haven't really got any money, I haven't got a house but I've got lots of children and that's what took all my money up. and I've got those to fall back on. I speak to most of them. yes I'm getting a bit nervous this year. and there's nothing – where is my career going, what am I doing. I'm at – I'm at that position this year now and I'm thinking oh I've got to do something. I need to make a change. this is the longest I've ever been in a job ((slight laugh)). this is the longest job I've ever had. you asked me what jobs I worked at before, I never stayed for more than two years, was the longest I stayed in any job. and then all the factories started to shut and you run out of places to work for ((laughs)) [. . .]

lines 640–3

> NI: I'll be lucky if I see my new daughter grow up to be an adult maybe. I am fearful of getting old. not middle aged but I am fearful of getting old and incapable of doing anything. (. . .)

lines 876–86

> NI: (. . .) I think everyone's different. It's terrible to be defeatist and conform to what everyone else wants you to be just for the sake of

conforming to a – to a concept to what you're supposed to be like at a certain age. ((unclear)). it's like – like a mini death. it's like dying before you're ready. self-imposed ((slight laugh)). and these sort of things should horrify me for some reason. that act your age thing it's a horrible thing to say to people. act your age because I am ((laughs)). no that's your problem – that's ehm. it's putting limitations on yourself. yeah. [...] it's sad. I feel sad about it.

There are two parts of the story in the first fragment: the story summing up NI's life and the story focusing upon his job prospects and history. Emotions serve the informant not only as the starting points of his stories, but in fact the basis of them, the narratives seem to explain them, account for them. He is getting nervous because he has no money, and so on. But despite these 'facts of life', the informant still chooses to put a stronger focus upon his emotions, his emotional experience of his life.

The emotional expression in the second and third fragments are completely direct. There is no attempt to 'soften' them, as in the first fragment by the use of 'a bit'. This time the speaker has no difficulty with talking about his fear or sadness. It is noteworthy that in the second fragment, despite beginning to speak of his daughter, the direct reference to him being fearful is not directed at anyone. He is fearful in his own right, so to speak: no relationship is involved. In the same way the sadness in the last fragment is directed at setting limitations upon himself.

Feeling about themselves

The last question to be tackled in this chapter is that of why men choose to speak of their emotions directly in some cases and distance themselves from their emotions in some other cases. Before I tackle the question in a formal way, I would like to offer a story.

Two days ago, while in my native Poland, I went to the physiotherapy clinic in the village where I am staying to receive some treatment. On entering the treatment room, I noticed a cane and a leather vest hanging on a chair and made a comment that someone must have forgotten to take them. The physiotherapist, a young woman of probably under 30, who showed me into the room explained that the items had been left by a man who was receiving treatment somewhere else. Indeed, a few minutes later, an elderly man, with very conspicuous difficulty in moving, came into the room to collect his belongings, apologising profusely for the intrusion. As he picked up his cane and began struggling to put the vest on, the female physiotherapist asked whether he needed any help, at the same time moving towards him and indicating her intention to help him put the garment on. The man, far from accepting the offer, stood up and said somewhat reproachingly: 'My dear, if a man can't [do it], he must pretend!' (*Moja droga, kiedy mężczyzna nie może, musi udawać*). He held out his hand, and instead of shaking the physiotherapist's hand, kissed it, said goodbye and left.

A note on the custom of kissing women's hands is necessary. A sign of chivalrous respect, still very much alive about 10–15 years ago, the custom is vanishing rapidly in Poland, and is now probably considered old-fashioned. In a medical or quasi-medical context, however, the action would be considered unusual and certainly marked. It would have most likely been seen as an attempt to shift the frame of the professional encounter on to a more social one, in which gender rather than doctor–patient relations plays a significant role.

I caught myself being surprised and fascinated by the scene: surprised because of the man's clear concerns to look manly and be perceived as such, given his age and disability; fascinated, because of his ability to encapsulate so well my thinking about the relationship of men's discourse of emotions to the dominant model of masculinity or, even more generally, the men's negotiation of the model.

I would like to account for the surprise, with which I felt quite uncomfortable the moment I thought about it. I think it reflected the view, shall I call it ideology, quite widely encountered in society (if one judges, for example, by the issue of *Newsweek* I referred to in the previous chapter) that masculinity is a matter of degree, especially with regard to age. The older a man gets the less of a man he becomes. This becomes even more pronounced, I think, when the man is disabled. In popular culture there are very few Inspector Ironsides, a disabled detective who used a wheelchair in a 1960s television series. With some humility I reflected that academics discussing problems of gender are not free from society's stereotypes and the prejudices they feed into. The modern masculine heroes are much more likely to be played by the likes of Jean Claude van Damme or Vin Diesel, with the ageing Arnold Schwarzenegger, Sylvester Stallone or Bruce Willis and particularly Clint Eastwood trying ever harder to protest their youthful masculinity. But even retreating to the positions of *Star Trek*'s sage-like Patrick Stewart as Jean-Luc Picard does not mean being so old as not to be able to move: Captain Picard still occasionally shows off his physical prowess, while implying the sexual one. And given that his and everybody else's physicality on the starship *Enterprise* is always overshadowed by the impossibility of matching Lieutenant Commander Data, an android, there is no risk to his 'real' masculinity.

Let me now explore the model of masculinity constructed in the short quip by the man I saw at my physiotherapy clinic. As I indicated, what he said describes aptly the relationship of the concerns of the local context in which a man operates within the requirements of the dominant model of masculinity. It refers to the social actor's need to translate the socially constructed requirements of what it is to be a man (the ideologies of masculinity, if you like) into his gender performance here and now. And this is where the problems begin, and this is where I have to have my fellow patient from my village to help me. The way I see the man's response is that he proposed to construct the requirements of the dominant model of masculinity in terms of pretence. In other words, it does not really matter whether you are the kind of man that society wants you to be, as long as you pretend to be. Or, to put it in a different way, it does not matter if you are *not* the kind of man the society wants you to be as long as you pretend to be. The performance of masculinity, the way society demands it, can be a pretence, a mask; not merely a performance the way Butler proposed, but an act, a strategy.

The fascinating bit of what the chivalrous knight with the cane said (well, implied) was that men are not necessarily what society wants them to be. And it is fascinating not because of this particular message: academics have known for a long time that there are various kinds of masculinity and various context-bound performances thereof. It is fascinating because the message comes from ethnographic evidence, from lived experience whose local concern was not an exploration of masculinity. Parenthetically, the short quip was also an interesting local construction of masculine identity. While the struggle with the vest was just about impossible to turn around, and the man's 'masculine face', so to speak, could not be saved, the quip protected him from what he perceived as the indignity of being helped. By explicitly taking on a masculine identity, he demanded to be treated as a man; or at least, he demanded that the physiotherapist, and perhaps I, too, played along with the game of masculine pretence.

I think this position on masculinity is also useful in exploring the way men talk about their emotions. The two super-strategies (speaking directly or distancing) are to do with the need to negotiate the dominant model of masculinity in the local context of interaction, and distancing offers a strategy to maintain the pretence of meeting the requirements of the dominant model of masculinity. The argument can be supported by my initial comments about distancing in relation to the strength of emotions. If the dominant model of masculinity is about control, the distancing strategies might help to maintain it. Thus the local concerns of masculinity and face and their relationships to emotion talk might engender distancing. In the local contexts of interaction, men might decide that speaking of emotions – particularly strong, dramatic emotional experiences – is unseemly for a man. This, together with the concerns of the positive face (Brown and Levinson, 1987), makes distancing strategies an ideal vehicle with which to maintain the appearances of masculinity. But this offers only a partial explanation, as it focuses mainly upon the distancing strategies, and accounts for direct emotion talk only negatively: speakers talk about their emotions directly only if they do not feel threatened in their masculinity. But that would imply that distancing strategies are in one way or another related to masculinity which, as I argued extensively in Chapter 1, is untenable. There is nothing 'masculine' about distancing strategies; they are not part of 'masculine language'. Additional explanation is needed therefore which will positively account for both super-strategies.

One of the systematicities I observed in the corpus was that when the interviewed men spoke of their emotions directly, their accounts tended to focus exclusively on them themselves, rather than on their relationships; on emotions the men felt themselves and for themselves, so to speak, rather than towards others. Alternatively, the distancing strategies were used to distance the speakers from emotions within their relationships, their emotions towards an Other. Consider the next example in which the speaker within seconds makes a shift from a distancing strategy to speaking explicitly about how he felt, the change coinciding with the change of focus from a relationship to the speaker himself.

Extract 21
CG, male, 1930, lines 469–78

> I: and what was your relationship with your parents like as you got older?
>
> CG: my relationship with my father was always close and loving. I was pretty devastated when he died. (.) then we had ((daughter)) and ((son)), I'd been married for seven years. that I suppose took some of the shock. but (.) for many many years barely a day went by (.) when I didn't think of him. and actually I still think of him on certainly a weekly basis.

Right at the beginning of his utterance, the speaker employs what I have discussed earlier as a distancing strategy in speaking of his emotions. He chooses to speak of the relationship with his father in terms of implied unspecified emotions, rather than focus on them directly. And yet, immediately after that, we witness a direct account of CG's devastation after his father's death. Note, importantly, that the shift is not merely that of strategy: it is, crucially, also a shift from speaking about an emotional relationship to speaking about himself in terms of his own emotions (even though clearly caused by the death of someone with whom the speaker was close). And indeed, the rest of his account again focuses upon his way of coping with the loss of the father, his marriage and the birth of his children being positioned as events that 'took some of the shock out'.

I can see an argument that CG responded with the focus upon his relationship because of the linguistic form of the question. The interviewer focuses directly upon the relationship, so the speaker responds with a similar focus. While valid, as I noted earlier in the chapter, I would not overestimate this concern for the following reason. I do not believe that questions, especially open ones attempting to elicit narratives, particularly within the context of an interview where the informant understands its purpose (this particular question was asked almost half the way through the interview), will be answered with strict response to the semantic component of conversational demand (on conversational demand, see Dascal, 1977; Holdcroft, 1987; also Sanders, 1987). A very similar question in extract 14 does not elicit an account focusing literally on the relationship, and a similar situation occurs in extract 15 (although the word 'better' could be seen as satisfying the interviewer's focus upon relationship). There are no grammatical matches there. The speakers choose to speak about their relationships in a different way. CG's response is part of a pattern that can be observed throughout the corpus. When men talked about relationships, they tended to distance themselves from their emotions; when they spoke about themselves and their emotions directed at themselves, they tended to speak of them directly. Of course, I do realise that I am not reporting on a quantitative study and that it is impossible to make some numerical claims about the corpus, and neither are such claims intended here. This is precisely why I am talking about tendencies rather than social or discursive 'rules'. I am reporting here on the typicality of a certain relationship, as perceived by the researcher.

So, finally, there are two questions that can be asked of my claim here. First, why should it be so? Why should men distance themselves from the emotions they have for others? Second, what consequences does it have for the models of masculinity? I think that the response to the first question must be made in terms of the stereotype of masculinity, the social requirements placed on men. As Jansz (2000) proposes, one of the focal attributes of modern masculinity is that: 'A man stands alone, bears the tribulations of life with stiff upper lip, and does not admit his dependences on others.'

Emotionality in general, but emotional involvement with others in particular, could be seen not only as losing the stiff upper lip but also as an expression of dependence on others. Distancing from such emotions helps maintain the appearance of part of the stereotype. But does this mean that men are as stoic as Jansz suggests? Nothing of the sort. They do have the emotions, they express them, and they do it in particular ways, in particular contexts. They put on an act to satisfy social stereotypes. It would be quite implausible to infer from such expressions the notion of inexpressive men (or men with restrictive emotionality, as Jansz puts it); implausible not only because the theoretical model does not allow it, but also empirically. Men do speak about their emotions directly, although they do it in different contexts. Somehow, in those contexts, their restrictive emotionality vanishes and they talk about how they feel. It perhaps seems that speaking of emotions not involved with others is more socially acceptable for men, less threatening to their locally negotiated masculinity. Incidentally, Shields (2002), drawing upon representations of masculinity in popular culture, proposes that there men do manly emotions which are much more controllable, more tame. But does it mean that I have just inadvertently come across a particular trait of masculinity, such that whenever men speak of relationships they tend to distance themselves from their emotions? Well, I do not think so and it is not because of the unrepresentativeness of the sample.

I shall offer a fuller discussion of the issue in Chapter 7; here I just would like to indicate my position briefly. Is there a white English heterosexual masculinity that can be characterised by such discursive patterns or practices? Well, I do not think there is any evidence that these discursive patterns are related to being a man in whatever form or demographic pattern. There is no such masculinity. The order is reversed: white, English, middle-aged (etc.) men sometimes use such strategies in certain contexts, probably for certain reasons which have their origin in the society's ideologies of masculinity. These discursive practices help men perform masculine identities. The question one can ask is therefore about the usefulness of certain discursive strategies/ practices in performing identities. In such a way one not only gains insight into men's identity activities – which are of course patterned – but also into the relevance of certain aspects of masculine ideologies. The discursive patterns are not indicative of masculinity, with certain characteristic patterns of behaviour and social action, including discursive practice. Such practice, for all we know, could well be used by white, English, middle-aged women, or Polish immigrants to Britain or whoever else. What they do show is that certain practices are used more often than others in social actors' repertoire. And if we could also assume that they are used in the performance of masculine identities, and I certainly cannot claim that the male informants always invariably spoke *as* men, the 'language of emotions' could shed some light on gender and masculinity in present-day Britain.

Models of masculine lack of emotionality are therefore no more than ideological resources for negotiating masculine identities, resources which can but do not have to be used and aspired to, among others by means of the strategies of narrating emotional experience. And it is this context-bound view of masculine identity that seems to me a very fruitful way forward in exploring what men are discursively up to.

Conclusions

This is the second chapter in which I have attempted to take issue with the existing models of masculinity. While in the previous chapter I showed that the lived model of masculinity can and does involve references to emotionality, here I showed that the notion of the inexpressive man is also quite problematic. I focused upon two super-strategies of emotion talk. I analysed ways in which speakers distanced themselves from the emotions they spoke about, and I showed that male informants also offered narratives in which they directly spoke about their emotional experience. The former tended to be used in narratives in which men referred to emotions towards others, while the latter were used in narratives in which they referred to themselves.

The dominant model of masculinity which assumes that men are emotionally handicapped, or that they are only capable of negative violent emotions, does not hold here. If anything, it might provide a resource for negotiating men's identities in certain contexts, such as men speaking of others, but it does not mean that the men speaking must avail themselves of these resources. Men – driven by the demands of the local context – can adjust the performance of their identities to suit the local context. This is why I am not trying to claim that I have discovered a new 'trait' of masculinity. Such a claim would mean falling precisely into the trap of essentialisation which I am trying to counter here. This is why I am arguing for a more context-sensitive approach to masculinity. I shall come back to the issues in the final chapter of this book.

In the next chapter I shall focus upon another aspect of men's emotion discourse. I shall investigate narratives in which men denied having certain emotions and will argue also that these stories contribute to the image of the emotional man and suggest men's 'emotional competence'.

4

'No Worries', or the Emotional View of Reality

Introduction

In the previous two chapters I have shown, first, that emotions are used in constructions of men themselves and masculinity in general and, second, that men speak of their emotions both directly and indirectly. In this chapter I would like to take the argument concerning men's ability to talk about emotions further. I set out to show not only their ability or readiness to speak about emotional experiences, but also their discursive awareness of such experiences and their ability to locate this within the discourses of surrounding reality. Thus, I would like to show that men's narratives show a certain 'emotional competence'. I shall demonstrate that, while being able to talk about emotions, men are also able to construct reality surrounding them in terms of the emotional impact it might have upon them. This includes, moreover, self-reflexive accounts of their own emotions. The final point about what I informally call 'the emotional competence' will be a discussion of narratives in which men view their emotional experience not only as something they are aware of, but also as something they 'manage'.

Possibility of emotions

In this section I shall discuss the ways in which men discuss the possibilities of their emotional experience, their awareness of the social expectations about their emotions and, finally, their ability to assess reality in terms of emotional experience.

Allowing emotions

One of the features of the presented narratives that struck me was the relatively large number of occasions upon which the interviewed men talked not only about having certain emotions, but also about *not* having them. This feature, I would like to argue, is, in fact, a confirmation of emotionality: it is a response to the implicit expectations of having these emotions. My argument follows from the assumption of Grice's Cooperative Principle and its four maxims (Grice, 1975). Grice argues that cooperative speakers are normally expected to be truthful (Maxim of Quality), informative (Maxim of Quantity), relevant (Maxim of Relation) and clear (Maxim of Manner). Saying that one does not have something can only be informative (and, indeed, relevant) if one expects the speaker to have it. There is not much point in saying that I don't play the Hoyt convention, if I am invited to play chess. By the same token, there is not much point in informing someone who invites me to play bridge that I don't play the Sicilian defence. Thus, saying that one does not have certain emotions can only be cooperative if the addressee expects the speaker to have them or, alternatively, expects that people in situations similar to those talked about might have certain emotions. In such a way, men denying that they feel something offer discursive insight into social expectations of emotional experience. In the following two examples, the interviewees volunteer information about not having certain emotions themselves, without the interviewer's putting the theme of emotions on the interview's agenda.

Extract 1
UT, male, born 1918, lines 556–68

> I: can you remember noticing first signs of ageing in you?
>
> UT: did I know the first time? oh well (.) to be quite candid (..) I've never known – well you do in – in your physical life. your life – it's hard to say but I – you being a young lady you don't like to say it really. but in life in general as you get older (.) your life changes. (.) but to me it's never worried me about that. and ehm as regards if I've ever felt anything. the only time as I've felt anything is like now I've engaged a cleaner. I feel fit enough to do but when I come to do it I can't do it. not as I want to do it. hoovering for instance.

Extract 2
SD, male, born 1922, lines 884–903

I: no I mean/what would you say from your own experience, when would you set the points in your life, I mean we have this working definition of forty to sixty, but I would like to know what you think were the goalposts in your life (.) what would you see as your mid-life phase which are the milestones which delineate it?

SD: mmh (..) well the big milestone obviously was when I came out of industry and went into the probation service. that was a complete change, that was a new way of life. (.) ehm when you had to think differently about issues because they were different, completely different. (.) ehm (...) that was a good time. it was a hard time but it was (.) a worthwhile time. I never regretted the change. (.) and then ehm (.) retiring. having some fantastic holidays like going across Russia by coach and to Western Israel (long time ago with) our study group (.) various other places, they were you know marvellous experiences. (..) and eh. but I (doubt) things just worked out, you know (..) some things you plan and some things you don't plan.

The two references to emotions are made with an implicit reference to the social expectations of certain emotions. These narratives show that there are certain events in one's life which are associated with certain emotions. Indeed in Chapter 2 I showed a few extracts in which men explicitly worried about the way they looked. And this is, I think, what UT implicitly makes a reference to. Men – or perhaps people – worry about their ageing process. Note also that the explicit reference to the interviewer is not in terms of her gender, but her age. The interviewee is an *old* man, the interviewer is a *young* woman. It is age that differentiates between them more than gender. Similarly, the reference to regret in extract 2 is an acknowledgement that radical changes in people's lives, or careers, do not necessarily work out. For the interviewee it has and he notes that by denying regret, something that might be expected after an unsuccessful change.

In the next extract, the use of a distancing strategy, or perhaps its reversal in that it is used to deny emotions, shows even better that the denial is made in reference to the expectation of emotion.

Extract 3
NE, male, born 1949, lines 303–14

I: and how did you experience the actual process of retiring?

NE: (.) I guess I'd been thinking about it for a lot longer than anybody else in the workplace knew that I had been thinking about it (.) so when it actually came I was totally prepared for it and ready and it wasn't a traumatic experience like some people experience it. (.) I didn't have a sense of loss, it was (.) you know in general in my life I never look back, I'm always looking to see what's what's coming up. and eh (.) once I had decided that I was going that was it. that's fine, that's no problem.

The declaration that the retiring was not a traumatic experience implies that it might have been. But the use of a distancing strategy, ambiguating the emoter, makes the potential emotion (which is also backgrounded) more of a universal potential. In other words, the speaker implies a social rule, one which has to do with emotions. This argument is reinforced by NE noting that a lot of people experience it in this way. The reference to not having a sense of loss could be seen as disambiguating the emotions behind the 'traumatic experience'. But the speaker goes even further: he gives an account as to why he didn't have those emotions. It is as if NE realises that just saying that he did not experience certain emotions might not be enough for the interviewer. Is it because the trauma behind retirement is so strong? So he offers an explanation of the way things are for him; he doesn't just say that he didn't have the sense of loss, it is because of the way he is, or perhaps because of the decision he takes not to look back. It is a way of managing potential emotionality, rather than a way of suggesting detachment from it.

The next extract is somewhat different in that the informant doesn't just deny having an emotion but, rather, he denies having the emotion of a certain strength (all the more implying, of course, not only the potential but actuality of emotionality). Also here the speaker offers an explanation for the strength of emotion he did have.

Extract 4
SE, male, born 1951, lines 335–41

SE: [. . .] you always have to have ehm a bit of a nagging doubt at the back with things like – with a major event like that. ehm (.) I've always had a certain self- confidence about ehm being able to see it through. so I was never completely depressed about the ehm redundancy per se, I was rather looking forward to the challenge of doing something about it ehm.

In this section I have talked about men's narrative awareness of the fact that certain events in people's lives (and their lives in particular) might be associated with certain emotional experiences and they implicitly acknowledge this by denying having these experiences. I have argued that such denials are in fact a confirmation of men's emotionality, at least implicitly, as the men do not construct themselves in terms of gender in these constructions. It is perhaps more apt, once again, to say that there are expectations on *people* to have certain emotions, and men are not an exception.

Emotionality of reality

In this section, I shall show a different aspect of this awareness of emotionality. I shall demonstrate that men can and do construct certain events in their lives as potentially or actually inducing certain emotional experiences. Put another way, men construct reality in terms of the emotions one might or might not have towards it. Such narratives situate their emotions not merely in the men's own world, but also in reality at large. In such a way I shall argue that men's local discursive performances are indicative of what I would informally like to call 'emotional competence'.

Before taking the argument forward, a note on the notion of emotional competence is needed, particularly because it resembles the famous concept of 'emotional intelligence' introduced in the bestselling book of the same name by Daniel Goleman (1995). Very briefly, Goleman's argument was that in order to be successful in modern life, people needed what he called 'emotional intelligence': the ability to understand other people's and one's own feelings and actions, coupled with the ability to control one's emotions, motivate oneself and others. 'Emotional competence', in turn, has been investigated in developmental studies. Saarni (1999) asked a question about judging maturity in terms of demonstrating self-efficacy in emotional interactions. The skills involved in achieving emotional competence involve the ability to recognise one's own and others' emotions or the ability to use the vocabulary of emotion.

Commenting upon or discussing such approaches or studies is beyond the scope of this book. They are fundamentally different from the approach to emotions or emotionality I have adopted here. I view 'emotional competence' as a characteristic of discourse, rather than a characteristic of people, their intelligence or personality (whatever they may be), or selves. My goal here is to show a particular feature of my informants' narratives, and to demonstrate that emotions are part of the constructed world view in men's discourses. At the same time I shall not be making, and neither do I want to, any claim about the informants themselves, their psychological characteristics or

dispositions. Also, I do not wish to lay claim to a new concept of 'emotional competence'; instead I would like to stress the informality of the notion. I see it as a 'shortcut' to describing certain elements of discourse.
Consider now the following extracts.

Extract 5
DQ, male, born 1957, lines 885–97

> DQ: [. . .] but I think it actually does (.) make you feel older but seeing this – this white – white hair – that – ehm – now I don't know whether that's ehm ehm stress or ageing or a combination (.) but certainly the guy that sits opposite me all day who's a year older than me has got white hair. So I suspect it might be the stress ((laughs)) but at least he's got hair ((laughs)). Ehm (.) it doesn't – it doesn't bother me (.) at all I – I'm not one of these people that ehm worries (.) inordinarily about (.) ehm any sort of physical loss of hair ehm I – it's – it's happening it will happen it will continue to happen I'll wear a hat in the winter and a hat in the summer ((laughs)).

Extract 6
ST, male, born, 1950, lines 1,169–76

> ST: I suppose really the next well – next big milestone will be a change of job or status or retirement. I suppose if people got promoted over me I might feel a bit resentful. which is worrying because the only way I can get promoted is to be promoted over people. there is that sense of well not my turn and why isn't it my turn because I've done the work. I deserve it anyway. the fact that they deserve it as well – strange morality.

While DQ assesses the changes in his physical appearance (both current and future) in terms of emotions, claiming that they do not and, implicitly, will not have a certain emotional impact upon him, ST in extract 6 talks about emotions only hypothetically. If something happened, he *might* have certain emotions. It is also noteworthy that ST realises both the potential emotional impact something might have upon him and the moral implications of his resentfulness. To make a pun of Seidler's words quoted in Chapter 1, it seems that he not only knows what is happening to him, he has words to describe it. This awareness can go even further. In a somewhat different example, in extract 7, the informant not only realises that certain events have emotional impact, but he also acknowledges emotional practices in society.

Extract 7
NI, male, born 1953, lines 876–86

> NI: (...) I think everyone's different. it's terrible to be defeatist and conform to what everyone else wants you to be just for the sake of conforming to a – to a concept to what you're supposed to be like at a certain age. ((unclear)). it's like – like a mini death. it's like dying before you're ready. self-imposed ((slight laugh)). and these sort of things should horrify me for some reason. that act your age thing it's a horrible thing to say to people. act your age because I am ((laughs)). no that's your problem – that's ehm. it's putting limitations on yourself. yeah. [...] it's sad. I feel sad about it.

There are two references to emotions here. NI says that the requirement of acting his age saddens him but, more importantly, he also notes that the breach of the expectation to act his age is associated with emotions. He refuses to be horrified by not acting his age. NI constructs a certain social practice in terms of what seems an emotional practice. Once again, the informant not only realises that for some people such behaviour might be associated with emotions, but also, by rejecting it, he shows awareness of his values as well as emotional experiences. But while NI rejects the social inevitability of certain emotions, the next extract confirms it. Certain situations in life lead, inexorably, to emotions. Consider the following two fragments, typical of the sample.

Extract 8
SD, male, born 1922, lines 277–92

> I: mmh (.) did retiring bring your age to the forefront of your mind? were you thinking, were you more conscious of getting older through retiring?
>
> SD: no I never thought about it. I was involved in so many things, I didn't had time to – ((clears throat)) like folks here who sit around all day and think about it but ((laughs)) I don't. I don't. ((unclear)) ehm, but it suits me here. I don't have to worry about shopping, I don't have to worry about the cooking. so I don't have to worry about that and getting on with other more useful things, you know. (.) whereas if I was still in the house – we sold obviously, which I sold (.) ehm (..) that's a tie isn't it really? looking after a house. (.) ehm I mean I enjoyed it all the time we were there but there comes a point when – you know. you move on, don't you? (.) if you want to.

lines 1,001–15

> I: and what comes to your mind when you hear of people being in their prime/ what do you associate with that?
>
> SD: in their prime? (.) I don't know. is that the fifties, I don't know ((laughs)) can't remember when I had a prime I don't know ((laughs)) what what age do you put the prime, fifties?
>
> I: ehm I am just asking you what you think
>
> SD: in the fifties. I don't know. never really thought of that (.) I suppose when you're in your fifties you know things are more settled aren't they you know (...) you don't have to worry about (.) quite so many things like houses and (.) ((muffled)) (whatever).

Even if one wonders to what extent the points about not having to worry about the daily chores are at the same time a forced argument to persuade the interviewer of the advantages of living in a retirement home, the construction of emotions and life is significant. SD constructs his alternative life in terms of something that would have a number of worrying aspects. The use of the verb *have to* makes the worrying, the emotions associated with the things the informant mentions, inevitable. One cannot not worry about all these little things in life. In the other fragment SD defines old age in terms of lack of worry; it is in middle age that one cannot but worry about a number of things in life. The emotions change with age and its social trappings (see also the ethnographic evidence provided in Hepworth, 1998), rather than the individual's ageing process.

In the next extract, the ageing process is contested as worrying, despite the interviewer's presupposition. Once again, we see an utterance in which the informant not only acknowledges some emotional traits in people (the construction is gender-free), but rejects the emotion as not applying to himself. Incidentally, the rejection is not a blanket one: there are other things that CL, and indeed others like him, find worrying.

Extract 9
CL, male, born 1922, lines 1,123–34

> I: and have you ever worried about getting older?
>
> CL: no. (.) I mean what is there to worry about? ((laughs)) there are only two certain things in this life: death and taxes, as you ((laughs)) (.) no I think some people do, I suppose some – well some people do worry like

that, I've never really worried about getting old. I mean I think it – you know (.) when you are old inevitably you worry about your health and (.) you see friends struck down with those ghastly things. and you – you do worry from time to time and wonder what's gonna happen to you. no but that's as far as it goes.

In both extracts above, the informants show age as impacting upon emotional experience (note also extract 14 in Chapter 2), or at least that with age people change insofar as their emotions go. Here we see ageing informants as worrying about different things as they grow older. But the point could be made more generally. These are not narratives in which the informants merely assess reality around them in terms of emotions. Their 'emotional competence' goes further in that their narratives construct emotions as changing over time. Not only certain events, but also age is associated with certain emotions.

In the next example, we see even more acutely that the change in emotional experiences can be liberating. Note also the shifts of the perspective between his own emotions and those which are typical of people of certain ages.

Extract 10
CG, male, born 1930, lines 77–96

> I: can you tell me in a bit more detail about what your life was like in this span – you know – your years between forty or sixty, is there maybe a particular point in that part of your adulthood when you were around forty when you would feel a new phase of your life was starting?
>
> CG: yes I can ((clears throat)) because (.) one thing of the legacy of my parents separating and my going away for school was that I suffered from very great insecurity – as I suspect lots and lots of people do – I think I had an inferiority complex. and although I always talked a lot I was in fact very shy. I used to worry terribly (.) what people thought of me. I think a great advantage of reaching middle age if you are a reasonably balanced person is that you begin to get all these problems into perspective. You cease to care so much what people think of you. you become your own master. and I've been very fortunate since I've suddenly realised that if people don't like me – well although I – I like to be liked – unless I've done something wrong to deserve their dislike I don't worry about it.

CG attributes the change in his emotional experience – from shyness and worrying to not caring – not so much to himself and his personal development, but to age. His change of perspective from speaking in first person singular to the impersonal 'you' – switching the narrative from that of an individual to that of middle-aged people – is still followed by another self-account. What happens in middle age generally, that one ceases to have certain emotions, has also been confirmed by his own experience.

I have argued in this section that men's narratives suggest an emotional competence, an awareness not only of their own emotions, but also of the emotions of others, of emotional practices and their associations with the social reality. By denying that they have certain emotions, men in fact confirm their emotionality, not only by suggesting the applicability of emotional experience to themselves, but also by suggesting that such experiences are socially expected. I have also shown that men's narratives construct reality in terms of the emotional experiences it might engender.

Choice of emotions

In this section I would like to take the notion of emotional competence further. I shall argue that in their narratives the interviewed men not only were able to talk about their past or current emotions but, importantly, they were able to account for them, accepting having had some emotions and rejecting having others. I would like to show that men narrated their emotional experience on a meta-level. The informants engaged in self-reflexive narratives in which they offered accounts of their emotions.

Emotions to choose from

To begin with, I would like to quote two extracts from a research on narratives of unemployment which I shall discuss in some detail in Chapter 6. Very briefly, after an interview session, the unemployed informants were asked to fill in a questionnaire gauging their experiences of losing their job and of unemployment.[1] One of the questions concerned what the informants felt on hearing about losing their job. The response consisted of a list of lexical labels (the emotions the unemployed person could have had) and a scale from 'not at all' to 'very much'. The questionnaire's instruction was to choose the appropriate emotions the informant felt and indicate the strength of the feeling. When the informants were asked to fill in the questionnaire, they were also encouraged to 'think aloud' while completing it and their comments were recorded. The following two extracts come from that particular part of the session. What I would like to show here is the ways in which two informants account for emotional experience. They narrate their experiences and seem fully in touch with them, engaging in some detail and subtlety in relating it.

Extract 11
JW, male, born 1957, interviewed in Opole, Poland

JW: anger [złość].[2] I got nerves.

I: what was the anger [złość] about?

JW: pardon?

I: what about?

JW: well that generally it has just passed. And the company could have continued. [...] so anger [złość] with those, the president, the [horse] yard in ((place name)). Fear? Not at all, what of? What should I fear?

[...]

JW: no despair at all, either. I am a bit resigned that for ten years one got close to all the people there. Yes, a little,[3] let's give two. Anger [gniew]. Mmh. It would have to be the same as in anger [złość], the same. In regret,[4] more like anger [gniew] because who can I be angry with? The president? The president is not listed here ((laughs)). No, one. Regret. It was disappointing to part, just sad. There was a lot of regret. Towards the employers, all these clever presidents.

Despite the fact that the informant is reading a questionnaire explicitly asking him about his emotional experiences and thus potentially influencing his choices, there are still two aspects of the account which cannot be easily associated with the questionnaire. It seems that the informant is able to relate the targets of his and presumably others' emotions quite well. Thus there is anger [złość] towards some people, there is regret directed at others. Admittedly, the targets of these two emotions can overlap. There is also quite a strong realisation of the appropriateness of certain emotions in the particular context. JW rejects the possibility of his anger [gniew] as something that does not arise in the situation. But he also realises that złość and gniew – the two emotions rendered by English 'anger' – are related and that for consistency he needs to make a similar choice in the questionnaire. Significantly, the informant related different emotions to each other, positioning one in the context of the other. Thus the reference to moderate despair (the notion introduced by the questionnaire, which I find quite strange as despair cannot, in my view, be weak or moderate) is anchored within the emotional bond he forged with his fellow workers. One emotion, it seems, stems from the other.

The appropriateness of emotions in a given context is evident in the next extract too, a more subtle, but also more ragged and full of hesitation, account of emotions like JW's. As he himself noted the subtlety of relating and understanding of what he feels, it is hardly a statement about a man's difficulty of understanding his emotions; rather, it is a statement of difficulty (human, rather than masculine, I would argue) in understanding a complex web of emotions in a difficult situation. This interpretation is reinforced by his last words, when he talks about understanding himself and his inability to continue without it.

Extract 12
WL, male, born 1960, interviewed in Opole, Poland

I: mmh. There was no anger [*złość*] at all?

WL: no anger [*złość*], because obviously that these, what am I supposed to get angry with, that this, I am to lose, that someone has hurt me, right?

I: mmh. Mmh.

WL: get angry that someone has duped me, this is the way I think. It's simply regret, because otherwise, it can't be fright.

I: and the regret? Can you tell me more about it?

WL: well, it's regret, I don't know, anger [*gniew*] I don't know. but not fury, just somewhere, and the regret that I think that way. It's very subtle isn't it? relating to what I feel, what I felt. That it could have been completely different. If it all happened, obviously there was regret, because if it had gone the way it should have, one would regret losing what one engaged in, right? Mmh. And the conversation would be different and different facts came out, right? I think that there is regret that it is a lost time, that obviously if there is work, then one can plans for oneself or something, I planned that things would sort themselves out, right? it can't be that one month, another, third one goes down instead of up, right? it's regret, because there is no cause for anger [*gniew*]. Perhaps I relate differently, explain to myself differently those, right? but I have to explain [it] to myself, if I explain [it] to myself, if I understand myself it will be different, if I don't manage it, it's hard to continue like that.

Having rejected feeling such emotions as anger or fright, the inform- ant's account focuses upon his *żal* ('regret') and this is the fragment of the extract which I would like to focus upon here. The emotions WL talks about are not only directed at different things in different times, but they are also located at different levels. Thus they are directed at the world, the lost time or lost plans, but also his emotions are directed at emotions themselves. WL regrets feeling such things (although his words, 'the regret that I think that way', are ambiguous and could be read as the regret about things that happened), he also regrets losing his commitment (*zaangażowanie*). The informant's emotional experience is also constructed in terms of understanding. He moves from very concrete and targeted emotions towards his more general emotional experience and ability to cope with the situations. WL appears to engage in self-management resulting in having or rather not having certain emotions (*gniew*, or 'anger') and it is the explaining he has to do to himself that can help him cope. His better self-understanding leads to better emotion management, leaving him better able to cope with reality, as the reverse is hard to ponder.

What I think we witness in the two extracts is not merely two men relating their emotions; I think the informants show a deep awareness of their emotional experiences, their social appropriateness, their location with regard to each other. Indeed, emotions do not just happen: it seems they have consequences (such as other emotions), or they are consequences. Moreover, what we could call the management of emo- tions is not a mere attempt to suppress them, to control the emotional experience. It is not an attempt to become a cold, unemotional man; rather, it is an attempt to understand oneself and from that understand- ing to reach a better ability to manage and live with emotions. But there is a more general theoretical point I would like to make here. I would like to stress again the problematic nature of the quantitative studies of emotions, especially by instruments such as questionnaires. The point was made forcefully by the constructionist approach to emotions which I discussed in Chapter 1. I would like to reiterate the point because of the nature of the data I have.

The argument that the critics of quantitative studies of emotions (see, e.g., contributions to Ekman and Davidson, 1994) make normally points out that the studies do not gauge much more than the readiness of respondents to use certain lexical items which, additionally, do not necessarily have counterparts in other languages. Agreeing with such a critique, I would like to add to the argument of the fantastic contextual complication of the narrative that the questionnaire misses. The informants not only tell us about their emotions, they tell us about who the emotion is directed at, which emotions they did not have. Admittedly, regret (Polish *żal*) directed at a particular person is quite a different emotion from that directed at the situation or the world, and which *żal* the informant chooses in the questionnaire is anyone's guess. By getting the completed questionnaire, one loses the wealth of lived experience constructed in the narrative, gaining relatively little. Without insight into that experience, emotions become labels, without much reference. It is in this context that I would like to present the final example in this section, an example in which the choice of emotion becomes also, to an extent, the choice of the label.

Extract 13
UT, male, born 1918, lines 606–30

> UT: [. . .] your – your life changes that way. (.) more so with a man than a woman. (.) yes you know what I am trying to get get like?
>
> I: I think so.
>
> UT: yes yes you would. but that – you find a difference there – but there again (.) you see that just in my case (.) didn't interest me at all because I know. to do that I'd got to go out. (.) and get in with somebody and that (.) you see? well if I would have started doing that like as I explained before, that comes first. (.) and it can be the ruin of you in five minutes. for the sake of madness for five minutes, can ruin you you see. so that – (.) naturally it crosses your mind it's only natural. but it never worried me. you see what I mean? never really upset me if you care to put it that way. (.) you see?
>
> I: what about signs of visible ageing like – you know getting – getting white hair or losing hair?
>
> UT: that don't bother me. ((emphatically)) oh no no no no that's (.) I could have no hair at all if I could go about and walk ((laughs)) wouldn't worry me, not in the least, no.

The choice between the worrying and being upset is to an extent one of the label. The informant's remark *if you care to put it that way* indicates the realisation that emotional experience can be constructed differently. The remark can also be used as lived evidence to refute the idea that what one feels is in one way or another non-negotiable, absolutely central to the label one uses to describe the feeling. One can only wonder whether this informant would have chosen the 'worry' option or the 'upset' option in the questionnaire.

The informant's last move can be a good summary of what I have been trying to demonstrate in this section. Men not only realise that things can have emotional impact upon them, but also that their emotions are related to the world in which they live. Accordingly, UT does just that: he situates his emotions in his social situation. Things, together with their emotional impact, can be put in perspective.

Emotional strategy

Men's narratives of emotions offer insight into the relationship between emotionality and the context in which the social actor operates. Emotions do not just happen; they do or do not happen because of a configuration of the social context. In such a way, in the extreme version of the construction, they can be controlled. The control, however, is not about not feeling, being cold or unemotional: it is about coping with oneself and the situation one finds oneself in. Thus, one could speak of the ultimate notion of the 'emotional competence', the ability to have an emotional (read: discursive) strategy.

In the first extract, the informant constructs his emotions as occurring only in a particular situational configuration.

Extract 14
FX, male, born 1931, lines 197–206

> FX: I mean I always played – I played golf. I've played sport all my life. I've worked hard I've obviously worked hard ehm I've been involved with a lot of public life. I've been on the bench over twenty years. I've been a Rotarian I – I've been chairman of governors at ((name)) school all those sort of things. I've never had time to worry about how old I am or how I feel. ((muffled)) I probably am getting to the stage now with doing less where probably I might start to think I don't feel quite so good as I used to.

Extract 15
DQ, male, born 1957, lines 938–54

> I: Do you observe people of your age who you kind of think are behaving in this ridiculous way?

DQ: Ehm (...) I – I haven't noticed. If – if somebody was doing something like that I would pick up on it certainly (..) I can – I can remember
somebody that I used to work with up to 10 years ago who – who (.)
wore this – full wig who was obviously totally bald and wore a wig. And it –
it was – you just had to stop yourself from staring at it really ((laughs)).
It's just not something that I could ehm (.) countenance ever. Basically
and yet this guy felt that he'd got this problem and yet now the (.) the –
the fashion really is that is to shave the head. Why worry about being (.)
bald? Why worry about it? Ehm but being fair-skinned I find that (..) it is
a difficulty in – in the summer so I burn. And it hurts ((laughs)). And I've
got quite a few straw hats ((laughs)).

There are two aspects of the expression *I've never had time to worry
about how old I am or how I feel* in extract 14. First, the informant
constructs business as precluding emotions, or at least the worrying.
Emotions do not happen, it seems, when you are really busy. Second,
and perhaps more interesting, the linguistic form of the expression
suggests the informant's agency over his emotions. It seems that the
informant could not have fitted emotions into his diary. But there is
a competing construction: *probably I might start to think I don't feel quite
so good.* So, on the one hand, the speaker constructs emotions as
something he has active control of, but a moment later, emotions are
positioned as a result of the situation rather than part of it: as life slows
down, he might begin to feel differently. What is interesting here is that
the informant's focus is not so much the control of emotionality that
enables him not to worry; it is, rather, all the other things that he does.
When he stops being so busy, the emotions might start creeping up on
him. The emotional strategy, therefore, is not so much about controlling
emotions (the second expression constructs them as beyond control)
but, rather, about a particular lifestyle.

Also the question *Why worry about being bald?*, in extract 15, suggests at
first sight that the informant asks about the rationality of having certain
emotions. The informant seems to question the sense of worrying, as if
one could take a decision not to worry. There is another, perhaps even
more significant, dimension of what he said. I think DQ's question is
more one of the impact a particular social situation should have. Should
baldness be seen as something so important as to merit the status of the
situation one worries about? It is not so much rationality of emotionality,
its sensibility, but it is the rationality of the significance attributed to
looking a particular way. The control over emotions DQ implies is
only partial, and it is anchored within the social status of a particular

situation: becoming bald. Change the status, and you change the emotions. But the implicit control, or at least some control, of what you worry about is more clear in the next extract.

Extract 16
SE, male, born 1951, lines 664–72

> SE: I wasn't thinking oh my god you know ((slight laugh)) what am I going do in old age if I don't have somebody with me sort of thing. that just didn't feature at all in my ehm in my thoughts, still wouldn't really. because there's so many other things that can happen I mean if you do marry and you know, your partner could die in the next year. that – that's what life's dishing out, just go and deal with that don't ehm don't worry unnecessarily about what might or might not happen.

Just like the men I quoted in the first section of the chapter, SE in extract 16 also constructs certain events in life as potentially traumatic, things that one might worry about. But the inevitability of this emotional experience is cushioned by the notion of unnecessary worrying. This is reinforced by the active form of going and dealing with what life dishes out which is carried over to not worrying. You might have to worry a bit, but not too much, not unnecessarily. You will be able to rein in your emotional experience at least partially.

What I am arguing here is the narrated awareness of a relationship between certain social situations and the emotional impact they might have. In contrast to quite a lot of studies indicating that emotions are culturally positioned as something to be controlled, here my argument is reversed. It is not about the controllability of emotions, it is more about the ability to reassess the social reality in which one lives. As I said above, by changing the reality, its social significance, you change the emotions. Note also that such narratives, without a more detailed discourse analysis than I am proposing here, might actually be used to postulate the model of the unemotional man, the man in control. However, the control in the narratives here is not, as I argued, directed at the emotion. The emotions seem to be a given, it is the reality that one might reassess. It is a different kind of control and a different kind of masculinity model. This argument is one about studying the discourse of emotional experience as submerged in its context, but also as a discursive practice with a certain socially significant lexico-grammatical form. Only then can one begin to appreciate the quite complex constructions involved in narrating emotional experience. Only then can one appreciate more fully that the apparent controllability of emotions, or men's alleged weak emotionality, might in fact be more to do with how social reality is constructed. This is not to say that the postulates of controllability of emotions in their cultural models are implausible. What I am proposing is that controllability with regard to emotions is probably a more complex and context-bound social construct, and as such it can only be studied in the full context of what people say and how they position their stories of emotions in their narratives of lived experience.

Conclusions

What I argued in this chapter is that men's narratives indicate what I informally call 'emotional competence': the ability to narrate the world in terms of the emotional impact it might have. This indicates the ability to see emotions as social, related to the world in which one lives. It also indicates the ability to narrate one's own emotional experiences reflectively.

In the next two chapters I shall focus upon how men talk about their emotions as part of some particular experiences they had. In Chapter 5, I shall discuss the way men talk about fatherhood and how they relate fatherhood to emotionality. In Chapter 6, I shall discuss the ways in which Polish men talk about unemployment. I see the two kinds of experiences – fatherhood and unemployment – as very significant for the modern man: fatherhood, with its discourses fluctuating between new fatherhood and men's inability to care for their children; unemployment, as one of the relatively new experiences which – as Faludi (2000) proposed – undermines modern masculinity on a scale unseen hitherto. Both experiences, I think, are extremely relevant to the discourse of masculinity, both public and individual. In both chapters I shall compare men's narratives with women's, although in different ways. In Chapter 5, I shall show how women speak of fatherhood, while in Chapter 6 I shall discuss how women talk about their own experiences of unemployment.

Appendix: originals of extracts in Polish

Extract 11

JW: złość na pewno. nerwy (dostałem).

OK: na co ta złość?

JW: proszę?

OK: na co?

JW: no tak że w ogóle to to że tak to tak przeszło i ta firma mogła przecież istnieć jeszcze. [...]. no to złość na tych (.) na tego prezesa, stadninę koni w Kluczborku ma. (...) lęk (.) wcale bo co tam czym? czego się miałem lękać?

[...]

JW: rozpacz też żadna. mnie już trochę słabo że (...) dziesięć lat to się człowiek zżył tam z wszystkimi ludźmi. tak słabo, dajemy dwójeczkę. (...) gniew. (...) hm (..) to by musiało być to samo. tak samo co złość co mnie (..) to samo. (...) to (.) w żalu, raczej gniew bo na kogo ja się mogę gniewać? na prezesa. a tu nie ma prezesa wyszczególnionego ((laughs)). (...) no jedynkę. ta: żal. żal było rozstać się no po prostu było żal. było dużo żalu. żal do pracodawców swoich, do takich mądrych prezesów [...].

Extract 12

I: uhm uhm. (..) nie było złości w ogóle?

WL: (...) złości to nie, bo to wiadomo że te, na co się mam denerwować że to to. ja mam tracić [na to że ktoś mi zrobił krzywdę jeszcze nie?

I: [uhm uhm

WL: denerwować się z tego że (.) że ktoś mnie w trąbę zrobił no to tak to właśnie tak to myślę że to nie tak nie? po prostu tylko żal no bo to inaczej (.) przerażenie to nie może być nie?

I: a żal właśnie? mógłby mi coś pan więcej o tym opowiedzieć?

WL: no żal jakiś taki na nie wiem to żal to (.) jakiś gniew nie wiadomo (.) taki no: ale nie wściekłość tylko po prostu gdzieś (...) no i żal że to akurat to (tak myślę) (.) takie delikatne to jest nie? ustosunkowanie tego co czuję (.) co czułem. no że to mogło być (.) zupełnie inaczej. jakby to wszystko było, no bo to wiadomo to był żal bo żeby to szło tak jak miało być no to żal tego utracić co się już (.) zaangażowało w to nie? (.) hm. (...) no i rozmowa była inna i: fakty wyszły inne z tego nie? (..) ja myślę że to: żal tego że (.) to stracony to ten czas stracony że wiadomo że jeżeli jest praca no to człowiek sobie jakieś sobie plany czy coś do tego tak jak ja sobie coś planowałem, że wszystko jakoś się poukłada, że to będzie dobrze nie? a trudno żeby jeden miesiąc drugi trzeci miesiąc żeby zamiast iść do góry to szło w dół nie? no to żal bo gniew to nie ma co, bo to (...) może akurat ja: inaczej odnoszę się, inaczej sobie tłumaczę te (.) niektóre te nie? ale to (..) sam sobie: muszę sobie wytłumaczyć, jeżeli ja sam sobie wytłumaczę jeżeli ja sobie sam siebie zrozumiem no to jakoś o będzie (.) inaczej jeżeli ja sobie nie dam rady no to trudno żeby tak było dalej nie?

Notes

1. This was a replication of studies presented in Makselon-Kowalska (2001) and Makselon (1998).
2. Polish *złość*, just like *gniew*, must be translated by English 'anger' (for a more detailed discussion, see Wierzbicka, 1999). As the informant deliberates one against the other, I decided to note the Polish words while translating into English.
3. A note on translation of the Polish *słabo* is needed here. The questionnaire the informant was filling in listed a number of emotions and asked the informants to locate their experience on a scale (hence the informant's decision to 'give two'). One of the options was *słabo*, translatable as 'a little', 'lightly'. But the first use of the word in the same utterance is quite ambiguous and I decided to translate it as 'resigned' because of the dative case of 'I' (*mnie*), although the form is quite unusual in the context. I suspect that the word was picked up from the questionnaire and incorporated into a form that it hardly fitted.
4. I decided to translate *żal* as 'regret' to render the fact that it was used in a nominalised way. However, the word 'regret' with its undertones of disappointment is not an exact match for *żal*, which also has a very strong dimension of sorrow, sadness. This is why the phrase *żal mi* – implicit in the next extract – could be translated as 'I am sorry', because of the dative form of *ja* ('I'), in the form of *mi* ('me'). It is yet another example in which we can see a mismatch of the repertoire not only of emotional vocabulary between languages, but also the grammatical forms through which emotional experience is rendered.

5
Emotions of Fatherhood

Data: We must say goodbye now
Lal: I feel ...
Data: What do you feel, Lal?
Lal: I love you, Father
Data: I wish I could feel it with you
Lal: I will feel it for both of us ... Thank you for my life

Star Trek: The Next Generation (The Offspring)

Fathers and emotions

In this chapter I am interested in the ways men position fatherhood in relation to emotionality. To what extent emotions are part of the discourse of fatherhood and the lived model of father involves emotional experience. But, as in Chapter 2, I shall also draw upon women's narratives and see whether one can find parallels between fatherhood as constructed by men (the insiders' perspective, so to speak) and that constructed by women.

It is not particularly surprising that, in parallel to masculinity, literature on fatherhood also assumes the model of the unemotional father. Indeed, Lupton and Barclay (1997) state that the emotional dimension of fatherhood has been underplayed by researchers. What little research has tackled the issue, say the two researchers, has dealt with fathers' difficulties in adjusting to fatherhood and so on. Fathers' alleged inability or reluctance to espouse fatherhood – and particularly its emotional obligations – has been commonplace in the literature. Coltrane and Allan (1994) point out ideals of fatherhood as unattainable to fathers, while Clare (2001) speaks of fatherly care as providing discipline rather than emotional nurture. There is literature on 'lost fathers' (Daniels, 1998) and 'absent fathers' (see, e.g., Lupton and Barclay, 1997), all referring in one way or another to what Pleck (1987) calls 'the distant breadwinner' (see also Tolson, 1977; Seidler, 1988; Rutherford, 1992; Morrison, 1993). Writers such as Lee say that fathers were not there for 'us', be it 'emotionally, physically, or spiritually – or at all' (Lee, 1991:xv; see also Biddulph, 1994). Even research that accepts fathers' emotional involvement in the family is predicated upon the model of lack of involvement. Cohen (1993), for example, assumes it is work that is the ultimate priority for men and thus they need to overcome it. In addition, there are arguments which lead to the construction of the fatherly role as redundant (Lyndon, 1993; Blenkenhorn, 1995). In the same vein, Stacey (1996) argues that there is little evidence that children need a male person so much as they need two caring adults. Interestingly, only older fathers are written about as having good emotional relationships with their (adult) children (for a review of literature on older fathers, see J. L. Thomas, 1994).

More recently, Shields (2002) discusses masculinity in terms of 'manly emotions'. She seems to reject the notion that men are incapable of feeling or expressing emotions; rather, she proposes, it is about talking about emotions. Men's emotions are said to be always under control, they are time-limited, context-driven and expressively economical. It is almost as if men are capable of switching emotions on and off as they please. Shields uses her view of controlled emotionality in considering fatherhood. She discusses the model of New Fatherhood in terms of doing the emotions 'the right way', the 'manly way' (see also Chapman, 1988). She continues her argument by saying that, while all sorts of spheres of life have blurred the distinction between genders (such as clothing, for example), emotions are one of the few areas where the gender boundary is alive and well.

Such models in their attempts to show all fathers in all situations, a fit-for-all fatherhood, do not and cannot reflect the complexity either of fatherhood or of masculinity, despite the fact that ethnographic evidence is quoted in support of such claims. Lupton (1998) reports that her informants talked about their fathers as emotionally distant. Similarly, Apter shows that adolescent girls talked about their fathers as the 'last person' to go to for emotional support (Apter, 1990). Even though, in a replication of the study, the findings are somewhat qualified, she still concludes that fathers are hardly relevant when it comes to emotions (Apter, 1993). And yet I propose that context-bound ethnographic evidence cannot provide legitimisation for a general context-free model of fatherhood.

It is much the same with public representations of fatherhood which, even though contradictory (see Lupton and Barclay, 1997; Sunderland, 2002), still focus upon the 'absent father', one who does not do the 'emotional labour' in the family or for the children (see, e.g., Lupton and Barclay, 1997; see also Coltrane and Allen, 1994; Böök and Penttinen, 1997; Lazar, 2000; Sunderland, 2002). Barker (2002) points out that control and distance are the central metaphors of fatherhood.

In a study of Polish and German literacy primers, Bennert and Galasiński (2000) show that the Polish textbook not only introduces children to quite fixed and patriarchal gender roles, but does it also in terms of emotions. It is only mothers who worry about children who are late home; fathers who are at home, on the other hand, are reduced to doing jobs about the house.

It is worth noting that such representations are reflected in fathers' own discourse. The website run by Fathers Direct (www.fathersdirect. com), the UK's national information centre for fatherhood, makes for sobering reading in that quite a lot of information there, together with the *fatherfacts* publication (accessible at the website at www.fathers direct.com/fatherfacts) seems to be geared towards disputing claims of irrelevant or unemotional fatherhood. Indeed, the publication and other pages of the website are at pains to dispel the myth that fathers are not emotionally involved with their children, which leads to perceptions of unfair treatment of fathers in British courts. Indeed, just before Christmas (on 19 December 2003) there was another demonstration by British fathers who protested against courts' discrimination with regard to their visiting rights, as they did on 19 May 2004 in the House of Commons.

I propose, however, that it is quite implausible to argue that public representations of fatherhood can easily be translated into lived models of masculinity (i.e., how men – and women for that matter – construct fatherhood) and, furthermore, how men construct themselves as fathers, or in their relationships with their children. It might well be the case, as I showed in Chapter 3, that such models provide men with resources for constructing their identities, but this does not mean, however, that they do so for all fathers, in all contexts, at all times. This is where I shall be taking issue with Shields's (2002) views, and indeed other models of unemotional fatherhood. I shall demonstrate that fatherhood can not only be constructed in terms of emotions, and sometimes, in fact, these are emotions over which fathers have no control. More importantly, I shall show that fatherly emotions can be constructed on a par with those of the mothers and that these constructions, signifi-cantly, are made by both men and women. This, in turn, will lead me to the problematisation of fatherhood and fathers' discourse. I shall argue for a more contextual understanding of fathers' identity and its separation from biological fatherhood. I shall finish this chapter with an analysis of narratives in which fathers talk about their households after their children have left home. This will allow me to introduce the notion of constructing emotions without recourse to emotion labels, which I shall explore in detail in the next chapter.

Fathers talk

Despite the kind of ethnographic evidence such as that offered by Lupton (1998), my male interviewees were quite happy to construct fatherhood in terms of emotionality. Fathers care and worry about their children. Emotions in fact are constructed as part and parcel of the condition of fatherhood; very often as far from being under control. Particularly interesting in this respect was the topic of children leaving home and fathers' feelings about it as witness the following example.

Extract 1
KI, male, born 1933, lines 507–21

I: and how old where you when your daughter left home?

KI: she left home – was it 36 – she left home eighteen years ago.

I: mmh. so how did you feel when she left home?

KI: ((exhales)) puh! exhausted. no (.) I felt relief really. if the truth isn't ((unclear)) from the fact that I didn't have to (.) think about it, about all the things about girls and what they get up to and what they don't get up to (.) I didn't have to worry about that. 'cause I think a father worries more about his daughter than possibly the mother would. I don't know, I don't know, I don't really know.

Let me continue with the analysis I started in Chapter 2. As I have already said, KI not only implies that he worried about his daughter, but also that there was really no choice in the matter. He had to worry, and this construction of worrying as a condition of fatherhood is continued when the speaker shifts the perspective between speaking about himself to fatherhood in general. Fatherly emotionality is constructed in very explicit agentive terms. There is no doubt as to their 'ownership'. Worrying seems a necessary 'action' of fatherhood: fathers do worry. And emotions become quite a powerful way in which to describe fatherhood. There is, it seems, no escape from emotionality, or at least the worrying.

It is in such agentive terms that KI compares fatherly and motherly worrying. It is fathers who seem to 'choose' to worry more. The comparison between fatherhood or motherhood is made in active terms of, I would say, caring. Fathers, at least as far as their daughters go, care more, are more active in it. The gender stereotype seems completely reversed. Worrying, fear in general, is definitely not men's domain. Men, if anything, are supposed to offer women solid support while they do the worrying. And yet KI is happy to construct fatherhood as more worrying. There is no evaluation involved: it is not as if fatherhood is better than motherhood. It is just a statement of fact (cushioned, incidentally, by the hedge 'I think', which takes away the certainty of a statement with full, unqualified, commitment). This hesitation is also rendered by the conditional 'would' used in reference to mothers.

The use of the singular seems to carry the universalism of the trait better than the plural, which is also underscored by the construction of the statement as more reasoned. The hedge 'I think' introduces the thoughtfulness of the statement. But the hedge has yet another function: the juxtaposition of the two parents' feelings – motherly and fatherly, with the fathers having the upper hand in worrying – seems to go right against the society's views on parenthood and its stereotypes. It is mothers that seem to be thought of as better carers. This is supported also by institutional practices: British courts seem to share such views, awarding custody considerably more frequently to women than to men (Geldof, 2003; Honigsbaum, 2003). In this context, KI's statement is somewhat safer. To recap, I am not arguing that the hedge softens the claim about the emotionality of fatherhood, but, rather, its juxtaposition with motherhood. Fatherly worry is constructed as a presupposition of the statement, a given. Neither do I believe that his repeated 'I don't know' at the end of the move is intended to undermine what he has just said. I take it instead to refer to the main point of his answer: the stopping of the worrying. In other words, he is not so sure that he has stopped worrying.

Emotionality as something inevitable for fathers can also be seen in the next extract.

Extract 2
SD, male, born 1922, lines 326–43

> I: you said ehm (.) it was – you had more freedom or less responsibility because you didn't have to worry about your children any more.

SD: not so much. well you always worry.

I: Can you remember when your children left –

SD: well you always – you always worry about them. ((unclear)) but (more) before they get settled down obviously

I: can you remember when your children left home, how you felt about that

SD: oh we were quite happy about it. (.) we weren't anxious about it or did resent it or anything like that. (time to let them go)

SD does not merely say that one worries when children leave home. He stresses it twice, as if there is nothing else to be said on the matter: you simply worry. The possible distancing strategy, the use of the impersonal 'you', has another function here, I think. Using it, SD describes the general principle to show this is the way the world is. Implied in the form is the fact that he is just a token example of the principle. He will always worry about his children. But the impersonal 'you' can, in view of the last turn of the exchange, be interpreted in another way. The speaker changes the perspective of his utterance and uses the pronoun 'we', most likely referring to himself and his wife. Although it could be seen as an extension of the wish not to speak about his emotions as directly, I think it more likely that it is an alignment with the mother of the children, a sort of gender-free construction of parenthood. One worries about one's children regardless of whether one is a father or a mother. I shall come back to this point later on. This particular construction can be seen quite frequently across the corpus. Men often positioned their emotions on a par with those of the mothers of their children. KI, with his construction of a father worrying more than the mother (extract 1) is very much an exception – however notable – to the general pattern.

Just as above in the case of SD, CL also constructs fatherly and motherly emotions as similar, as shared by the two people.

Extract 3
CL, male, born 1922, lines 159–67

I: so how did you feel when your children were leaving home? did it affect your life?

CL: well, ((sighs)) how does anybody feel when their children leave? you miss them ((laughs)) (.) but ehm I don't think it affected our lives a great deal. I mean we didn't say 'hurray! children are gone, we'll get a smaller house, we'll do this, do that and the other' I don't think affected us in that sort of way.

CL also begins with an impersonal construction of the feeling rule, except that this time the emotion is missing them, rather than worrying about them. It is a means of positioning himself as someone espousing the rule. The construction of 'missing' one's children as a rule only adds to its naturalness. 'How else can one respond?' the interviewee seems to be asking. And the form of the question – similar to the 'Is the Pope Catholic?' kind – augments the obviousness of the missing even further. Incidentally, this kind of argument opens a new possibility as regards interpreting distancing strategies. The dissociation from direct ownership of emotions, so to speak, could be to do with the fact that the constructions speakers use can be made to refer also to other people (such as their spouses). In such a way, the distancing strategy offers the possibility of keeping the option of sharing emotions open. This can also be seen in the next extract, even though the emotions themselves are quite different.

Extract 4
ST, male, born 1950, lines 1,020–31

I: so summing up what would you say is middle age for you now?

ST: well I'm not conscious of being middle-aged I said that right at the start I mean but in so far as I am in the middle of my age if I'm in the mid-dle of the three score and ten – well it – with luck it'll last me a bit more than that erm (.) it's perhaps the – at this point it's the slight frustration of knowing the children are still there and still need to be looked after erm and yet ((wife's name)) and I want to start having our own lives erm. so there's a slight frustration. erm perhaps a slight frustration. [. . .]

Despite the explicit construction of two separate individuals in terms of 'we', the informant and his wife want to start their own lives. The separation of the perspective is augmented by the plural 'lives' suggest-ing that the two married people may not want to share life after the children have left. And yet the distancing strategy allows the informant either to hide the differing perspectives of the children or to imply that the emotion of frustration is in fact shared. Either way, the way ST constructs the emotional attitude towards the children does not involve separate emotions, separate perspectives. It seems that whatever the outlook upon the rest of life, the two married people share their attitude towards the children, even though this is a frustration with the situation, or should I say, 'parental emotions towards the children'. I shall come back to the issue in the section on constructions of the family home below.

Mothers talk

In the previous section I showed that men's narratives not only positioned fatherhood in terms of emotions but also, significantly, put it on a par with motherhood. The speakers constructed their emotions towards their children as shared with their wives, occasionally blurring the gender difference or, to put it differently, constructing the identity of parent, rather than father. But fathers' narratives of fatherhood elicited by interview questions cannot be seen as merely an account of the fatherhood experience. While guided by the usual truth bias or, put another way, the Maxim of Quality of the Gricean Cooperative Principle (Grice, 1975: i.e., the social expectation of truthfulness), what the interviewees say is also subject to the local considerations of face (Sarangi and Slembrouck, 1992). In other words, one cannot expect the interviewees to flog themselves in front of the interviewer and admit to all the mistakes they made in their attempts to bring up their children, and to their emotional coldness on top of it. Their local-context construction of fatherhood identity will also be subject to pressure coming from a more global context of both fatherhood and motherhood stereotypes. Fathers speaking of their children are more than likely to draw upon discourses of good fatherhood and motherhood, the latter also given the public discourse of mothers' apparently greater natural skill at handling children. In other words, the point of fathers' accounts of fatherhood is that they are insiders' accounts. Interestingly, however, they are seconded by those of the interviewed women.

First, some of the interviewed women chose to describe both their fathers as well as their husbands in terms of emotions.

Extract 5
KO, female, born 1907, lines 296–308

> I: so what about your parents, did you look after your parents when they were old?
>
> KO: well (. . .) I looked after my father. he used to love to come to ((place name)) (.) he came for weeks and I mean weeks at a time. he loved being here, I loved having him and he enjoyed – he was a widower by that time.

he enjoyed being looked after. he was never any bother. never never. he enjoyed being looked after, he enjoyed his meals. he was ehm – he played ball. he was very good at footy but he never played here. ((unclear)) I used to wonder why he didn't join one of the clubs here because he was very good at it. you think all these things and it's too late.

Extract 6
EI, female, born 1911, lines 379–88

I: But how did you feel about the age difference between you?

EI: Well I think I felt it a bit at first. you know I used to think ehm – because he loved children you see and he loved my grand children and he used to play with them [. . .] and I used to say – there's no use – I can't have anymore you know that. well he said we could adopt one. He'd never had any children you see and he just idolised my two grand children.

As I already signalled in Chapter 2, KO – in extract 5 – describes just about the entire relationship between her and her old father in terms of emotions, mostly her father's. There is, however, one reference to the informant's own emotions in that she says that she loved having her father at her place. I would suggest that it was said as if to pre-empt potential suspicions that the daughter was not particularly happy with the looking after she had to do, that her father was in fact a burden, an old man imposing himself on the younger generation. The reference to her own emotions precludes such suspicions. Thus, apart from this one exception, their entire relationship is narrated through mental clauses referring to KO's father's emotional states. Interestingly, the father's perspective is maintained also when a potential reference to her own negative emotions is made: *He was never any bother*, which is another statement made just in case. It is the father's emotions which are chosen as the medium through which we see the reality.

In extract 6 the question about the age difference is changed into EI's husband's attitude towards children. His love of his wife's grandchildren seems to be the basis upon which the relationship is constructed. The narrative is dramatised by the interviewee accessing her own past voice and playing out the conversation she might have had with her husband. Significantly, her inability to have children is never positioned as a problem and neither, by extension, is his love for children. The emotions through which EI's husband is constructed are only positive and constructive. The construction of emotional fatherhood in women's discourse does not end here. Similarly to men, the women also position their husbands'/fathers' emotions on a par with their own (see below).

Extract 7
ND, female, born 1911, lines 677–87

> I: but what about when they first went to college? how did you feel when they were leaving home?
>
> ND: oh it wasn't very nice. we missed them terribly. my husband was alive when the girl went but not when the boy went. (.) and eh (.) well he took her to college. and we went up whenever we could. 'cause she made friends with people, and we were able to stop with their parents. (.) but it was a big gap when they went. 'cause she used to play the piano and she was always working, she was in the guides. we've always been very busy, all of us.

Extract 8
QM, female, born 1946, lines 472–93

> QM: (...) we're all going to America together as a family to see the young one, which was instigated by the older one who is now nearly twenty-five. he said come on let's all go to America and see ((name)) and we said oh don't know whether we can be bothered and we said you book it and we'll go and he did book it and we're all going out – going out together. so ehm no I don't think we mind at all that the boys are not home permanently. we wouldn't like to think that they didn't come home but because we know that we – people are asking us now you've got – they're saying you've got a big four-bedroomed detached house are you moving? I'm going to put a banner outside saying no we are not moving because we like the space, we like the area, and all our friends are here and we want to keep a room each for the boys until they buy their own property. whether they get married or not of course people don't get married these days do they ((slight laugh)). but unless or until they move out completely and buy their own homes, we want to keep rooms for them so you know we're quite happy at the moment that they're not living at home permanently but we know they'll come and go so.

In extract 7, ND begins her answer with an account of both her and her husband's emotional response to their children's leaving the family home. There is no hesitation, no qualification; the emotion of missing is shared between the two partners. There is no attempt to distinguish between them. They both missed their children. And immediately after the account of the shared emotions, ND changes the perspective of her narrative and begins the story of her husband taking their daughter to college. This introduction of the new perspective reinforces the interpretation of the relevance of shared emotions. The interviewee very clearly chooses the perspective she wants to use for her account. The joint 'we' perspective is not the 'default' perspective through which she tells family stories.

In extract 8, just about the entire utterance of the interviewee is made through the 'we' perspective. The informant is very clear in constructing the parents' perspective on the rest of the family. There is hardly a mother, hardly a father. There is a 'we', a couple who, in terms of emotions, are not fussed about going to America, or who are happy to be on their own without the children. But it is also the 'we' who do not want to sell the house or who want to keep the bedrooms for the children. The only time that the interviewee constructs herself as a doer is when she talks about putting up a sign that the house is not for sale (a metaphorical way of reinforcing, interestingly, the 'we' perspective).

I do not think that the statements about keeping the bedrooms for the adult children are statements about the current or future layout of the house and its furnishings; it is a way of showing attachment to the children, albeit indirectly. The statement is aimed at constructing the 'family home', a place where the children have their anchor, a safe haven, the place where (at least until they set up their own families) they have a home. The informant constructs the family home in two ways: in terms of physical space which cannot be changed at will and in terms of both parents' wish to keep the home open for the children. But at the same time, there is a certain acceptance of the state of affairs: the informant realises that she is talking about the natural course of events. Stereotypically, I think, this emotional attitude towards the physical space, the narrative of home-making, should be the woman's domain. It is women who are socially thought of as home-makers, as those who are also the family home-makers (Dunscombe and Marsden, 1995, 1998). Indeed, there is much evidence that it is women who spend considerably more time on childcare and, more generally, on household work (Hochschild and Machung, 1989; Coltrane, 1997). And yet I would like to show in the next section that it is also men who construct the family home in their narratives, one which they have an active part in making. The lived model of masculinity once again encroaches upon the supposedly feminine areas of life, partly probably also in reflection of the changing patterns of gendered division of housework (see, e.g., Sullivan, 2000; also Whitehead, 2002).

One last comment upon QM's turn. Her statements about the family home are surrounded by those telling us about the couple's emotions. I think the interviewee's utterance can be interpreted as one of a contented wife and mother, someone at one with her husband, with whom she shares both the emotional outlook on the family's business but also the way she thinks about the family, and even the way she plans – perhaps emotionally – the way her family's house is arranged. Such contentment, I think, will be manifest in at least one of the home-making narratives of my male informants.

Family home

In contrast to the stereotype of the absent male uninvolved in home-making, in their narratives, my informants positioned themselves very clearly as co-makers of the family home. Just as in extract 8 above, there is a clear pattern of intactness of the family household and its physical space.[1] But, at the same time, all the narratives are full of understanding of what happens. The 'empty nest', however traumatic it is, is also understood to be inevitable. The most frequent construction of the family home is done by implication: the family home, or its disruption (potential or actual), was constructed when the informants talked about the children moving out. Consider the following two extracts in which the informants speak of the disruption with increasing strength.

Extract 9
IF, male, born 1947, lines 413–27

I: and how do you feel about your son moving out?

IF: ((son's name))? (.) I don't think he'll move. ((laughs)) I don't know. last year as I say we went away last September for our wedding anniversary and spent a week, fortnight on our own. (. . .) weird that (.) weird. it took a bit of getting used to. (.) ehm (.) so I would imagine if ((son's name)) got married and moved out it would be the same thing, it would take a bit of getting used to. eh depending on where he'd move to (.) so you know as far as ((unclear)) goes – we never moved far away from our parents. ehm (.) well obviously ((daughter)) and ((boyfriend)) with the job he has got now, possibly moving – they could be moving into another country. (.) might take a bit of getting used to that. (.) we're pretty close really.

Extract 10
WC, male, born 1926, lines 346–56

I: mmh can you remember what it was like when your children left home?
WC: ((clears throat)) very quiet, very quiet. yes we – it was eh (.) eh (.) it
was like living in a mausoleum. although – they both lived in the same
area. and so we saw them quite a lot so that sort of softened the blow
((unclear)). and of course there were compensations as well. because
when they were teenagers and they were out late eh (.) nobody went to
sleep until they were in and things like that (certainly).

IF, in extract 9, extrapolates his and his wife's experience of being on
their own away from home based upon the possibility of his son's moving
out. In contrast to his own experience of not moving far from his and
his wife's parents, he also realises that his son might move further,
something which is undesirable, and accepts it would be difficult. However, IF is still talking about something that has not yet happened.
He has not yet experienced what WC (in extract 10) and other male
informants talked about: the quietness of the house after the children
are gone. He is still ready to translate the experience of having children
leave the family home into a new quality of the space they lived in.

WC's account is quite graphic in its description of the house as a
mausoleum: a place of sombre silence, a place with not much life. But
this physical space of family home is also rendered by the final words in
his move. This is the place where no one slept when waiting for the
children to come back. The family home, as in the narrative of KO, a
female informant (extract 8), is constructed as a safe haven, a place
where one is waited for. The perspective WC adopts is that of the family,
more likely to be the adult part of the family: the parents. The reference
to nobody sleeping while waiting for the teenagers to return home is as
much to him as it is to the other part of the 'family', his wife. WC partakes
fully in the family worrying about the children.

In the next extract, the loneliness and the trauma of being left by the
children, once again shared between both parents, is constructed also in
terms of the home space.

Extract 11
EX, male, born 1926, lines 362–79

I: [. . .] now do you remember when your children left home? how did
that take place?

EX: we missed them when they went out to work you know. ((name)) worked in a hotel [...] ((name)) became a solicitor and she's done very well now.

I: and how was it for you and your wife when the children were gone?

EX: bit kind of lost.

I: in what ways?

EX: well you in the mornings you see ((name)) would get up and you miss that you don't see them. ((unclear)) she's left home now she's working. you forget that at the time. she comes and sees us once a week though [...]

In quite a dramatic account of shared missing for the children who moved out, EX in his last turn changes the perspective from explicit emotions to the experience of the empty home. This time it is not the quietness of the place, but the experience of lacking an element of the household. The reference to forgetting that the children moved out carries the implication of the naturalness of the children being at home. Children who leave home leave a hole in the lives of the parents; once again, EX does not even attempt to construct separate perspectives for himself and his wife, because all the missing, all the forgetting, all the not seeing is shared by both parents. Gender lines get blurred completely. In the next such example, IF goes even further in not only making a reference to the trauma of taking his daughter to university, but also tells the interviewer about the decision to leave the house as it is, as if the daughter had not moved. She still belongs to the house, to her place. Implicitly, the same kind of message is given by CL in extract 3, above. CL rejects the possibility of selling the house and moving somewhere else, at least for now.

Extract 12
IF, male, born 1947, lines 386–404

I: and can you describe what it was like when your daughter moved out?

IF: well (.) permanently (.) it sort of crept up on us. I mean the night we left her at university (.) she didn't go in halls, she went into a student's house. and that night was pretty traumatic, the drive back down the M6 was pretty dramatic. (.) so we've been used to her not being here. (.) for the last three years, and she's close enough. it's only 40 minutes up the motorway for her to come home for a weekend or whatever. and she has done. so (.) it's hard to say that she's left home. her bedroom is still up there. She's got the biggest bedroom. eh ((son)) poor lad has the small bedroom. (.) but we will not change that and let him go in there until she is married. Once ((daughter)) is married as far as we're concerned that's it. 'cause it is now, she is still – this is still her home. And they comes regularly and her boyfriend comes with her. he goes on the couch-bed downstairs, and she is up in her bedroom so –

Despite the trauma of the drive and leaving his child at the university, spatially, IF's daughter has not yet moved out. Her safe haven is still there, and this is what IF explicitly says. Linguistically, the extract is interesting because of the shift of perspective between the narrative in terms of the daughter's right to *her* bedroom and the parents' decision not to change it. This is an account of the status quo and the decision to keep it. And it is the change in the family home that will mark the daughter's leaving, rather than her actual moving out. Despite her departure for the university, it is almost within her parents' gift to decree whether she has left or not. And it is the parents' perspective, rather than her mother's or her father's, separately or together. It is 'we' who decide. This belonging to the family home is reinforced by the account of the daughter's visits home. She goes to *her* bedroom, while her boyfriend has not got a space in the house. One could of course wonder to what extent this fragment also has a moral undertone: is it also a construction of a decent family? This, however, is outside my interests in this chapter. But as much as IF boldly decides on the cutting-off point being the daughter's marriage at which time she will lose her space in the house, such a decision in the next extract is shown as being a bit more difficult.

Extract 13
WC, male, born 1926, lines 99–115

> WC: ((clears throat)) well I don't wanna be seventy-three. I mean (.) since I am retired now we've got a house in Spain – I bought a house in Spain, so –. and this is why we bought this – this apartment. I lived in a four-bedroom house, and I lived there for thirty years. and it was a very very nice house. it was a large house (.) that's where my children grew up, that's where we had parties, we had wonderful times and suddenly – I mean the children, they've all gone they've all been out for years I said 'well what am I doing living here'. I only need a third of the space. and I don't wanna spend my time (.) shovelling leaves and gardening any

more. so I stopped doing that. we sold the house, we bought this one. and we intend to spend more time in Spain eh in the nicer weather eh driving around. and that's where (we should be). (.) so middle age didn't really come into it for me. before I knew where I was it was old age. ((laughs))

The beginning of the story is that of constructing the home as a family place. This has changed (suddenly) with the children moving out, a disruption of the family life. But the main point that I would like to make here is that WC keeps the house for much longer than necessary. It is only after years, as he says, he decides to move house. But the decision seems to be based upon not needing the house, all the space in which his children had grown up. In fact, just before the interview, while the interviewer was taking a life-course summary, the informant did explain that the move from the family home was because 'the house was too big without the children'. But then in the extract here, he complements the reason. This time, it is not wanting to do the jobs about the house. This narrative is different from the others in that the informant more clearly constructs his own perspective in parallel with the joint one. However, it is the 'we' perspective that is used in reference to the family life (the wonderful times in the house). The decision to sell it, on the other hand, was based upon his not wanting to do the garden work, yet the act of selling, again, was joint.

The final point I would like to make here is that the narratives of the 'empty nest' have their counterpart. There are a few instances in which the concerns of the family home are overtaken by the concerns of the 'normal' course of events and the need of the children to actually leave home and start life on their own.

Extract 14
ST, male, born 1950, lines 400–14

I: how do you feel about your children growing up and leaving home?

ST: I wouldn't say we can't wait although sometimes you think you can't wait (.) I mean – you do notice them getting bigger and older and in fact it's been very noticeable for the past year I suppose in how keen they are in taking more control over their own lives which sometimes means making more demands on ours. (.) it's about time that they went – well that John went. he's old enough now. he needs to break away. I mean he was away last term. he was missed and then he came back and he's been back since. it's been very strange. you get used to them being away. and then they come back and it's permanent not – not just for a vacation.

Extract 15
CG, male, born 1930, lines 409–26

I: what was it like when your children left home?

CG: well (.) I know I'm tempted to say they really never left home. ((daughter)) is the one who left home first (.) but she's regularly here with the children (.) oh once a week ((wife)) goes over to ((daughter's place)). which is about thirty miles away, about once a week. so we see her – and she was in Wales with us last week – we see a lot of her. ((son)) (.) left home because we kicked him out (.) we felt that he had to stand on his own feet, and he wasn't. eh he wasn't anxious to move. we persuaded him he ought to buy a flat while the market was right. (.) so he bought a flat. but then when he sold it he came back to us. and came back to us for another two years. until finally he wanted to buy a house. and he's just down the road, a mile down the road. and finally he got married, which was (.) five years ago, four years ago. (.) and he also lives just down the road.

Both informants construct a need for their sons to leave the family home, with the first speaker also making a reference to the emotional experience of the event, which, eventually, yields to getting used to the fact. The two accounts are quite different, though. While ST constructs most of his narrative though his son's perspective, most of what CG says about the process of reaching the decision to leave is through his and his wife's eyes. It was they who kicked him out, they who felt the son needed to stand on his own feet, they who persuaded him to buy a flat. Moreover, despite the fact that the process of kicking CG's son out is not explicitly constructed in terms of emotions, I would suggest that his narrative actually is. It is of course impossible to give the emotions a label with any certainty (CG does not use one), and analysts cannot simply take over. Still the narrative is full of caring, of parental concern for the welfare of the children. And it is the 'we' perspective, I think, that helps CG construct it. CG and his wife are positioned as the caring parents; they are constructed to take active parental actions for his son. This action is anchored not only within the reference to the 'natural' course of events (the son had to stand on his own feet), but also by references to the market being right. Furthermore, the 'kicking out' has worked only to an extent in that the son was allowed to come back home until he decided to buy a house again. There is no father, no mother; there is just a 'we' joined in its relationship with the child. There is no hesitation, no hint that the perspective might actually consist of two separate views. The parental 'we' is fully united. My argument here is that despite lack of emotive language, or reference to any emotions, CG implies his and his wife's emotional experience in the way the story is told. I shall argue that point in detail in the next chapter, when I discuss narratives of the unemployed and what I term their 'discourse of helplessness'.

Fathers' discourse?

The last extract, along with most others here, is quite significant for understanding fatherhood, father's identity and father's discourse. On the basis of these I would like to suggest a more radical contextualisation of these phenomena. I think that the positioning of men's and women's emotions, and other family activities (as, for example, in extract 15) as shared by the two partners not only suggests a radical dissociation of biological fatherhood from the social but, more importantly, from father's identity or subject position. The fact that a biological father speaks to or of his biological children does not mean that he takes on the identity of the father.

Recall now Shields's (2002:117) recent example introducing her considerations of masculine emotionality. She describes a scene of a sportsman who, during an American football match, picks up his nine-year-old son and kisses him on both lips and cheeks. The scene is picked up by a television commentator who relishes the kisses from a man to a boy and back. Neither the commentator nor Shields when recalling the event and the commentary at the time have any doubt that the scene is all about, first, masculinity and, second, fatherhood. Shields speaks of the fatherly tenderness, calling the kisses a 'nurturant, loving display'. While I am not going to comment on the interpretation of a sportsman's emotional outburst in terms of nurturing his son, which seems to me rather overinterpreting, I wish to argue that the uncritical interpretation of the scene in terms of fatherhood is quite problematic.

The data I presented above show that there are contexts in which both men and women construct themselves and each other as adopting the gender-free identity of a parent. The female speakers in extracts 5–8 make no distinction between fathers or mothers or their emotions. There is no hesitation in taking up the joint parental perspective. And, importantly, it is not a family perspective; the speakers very clearly speak of their children so if it is the family speaking, it is the parents' side of the family. Significantly, the explicit emotional perspective in extract 8 is intermixed with a statement of parental contentment with the children's achievement. The 'we' in extract 8 never gets separated when it comes to the issues of family, even though the speaker happily speaks of herself putting up a 'not-for-sale' banner. Neither the men nor the women speak of fatherhood, even though they clearly could, and even though the individual perspectives permeate those of the 'we', of the parents.

Shields never stops to ponder whether the emotional display she witnessed on television could be to do with something other than gender or fatherhood. Could it not be a happy sportsman who picks up his greatest fan?! Shields's assumptions are based upon the fact that she saw a biological father picking up his biological son. But, if it is stating the obvious that non-biological fathers can make excellent father-figures (or, to all intents and purposes, excellent fathers), there is no reason why this argument cannot be taken the other way round. A biological father does not have to always be a father in his actions. The men and the women whose narratives I analysed here are quite clear about it. They construct a different identity for themselves: the identity of a parent. It is an identity that takes away the issue of gender from the relationship with a child. One could of course wonder to what extent certain other aspects of masculine performance, such as clothing, after-shave or facial hair impose gender right back into the relationship (in other words, to what extent the child still perceives, say, the person with the beard as necessarily the father). But such considerations are outside the scope of what I am trying to argue here. My argument is that the fact that the biological father says something about himself and his relationship with his child, or to his child, does something to the child, does not make it a father's discourse, or a fatherly display of emotionality, or anything else fatherly for that matter. It may well be that a parent (who happens to be a biological man) is saying something, doing something, but it also may be someone else: a playmate, a coach, a lecturer, a spectator. Indeed, Morgan (2001) suggests that family might not be a site of gender work only, allowing also the possibility of 'de-genderisation' of parenthood (see also Lawes, 1999).

Such considerations have, I think, a number of theoretical consequences insofar as both gender research and fatherhood research are concerned. They not only problematise the notion of gender as an all-encompassing dimension of social reality, but also problematise fatherhood research. One cannot, I think, claim that one analyses fathers' discourse just because one records biological fathers' narratives. Fatherhood is a context-bound identity. One constructs or performs fatherhood just as one constructs other kinds of identity for oneself and there is nothing given about fatherhood in relation to one's children. I shall explore these points in some more detail in the final chapter of the book.

Conclusions

In this chapter I set out to show that fatherhood can be constructed in terms of emotionality. I showed that both men's and women's narratives do it, with fathers' narratives being constructed in terms of their emotional attitude towards children. I also showed that these narratives constructed men's emotions on a par with women's, actually blurring the boundary between men and women and constructing a category of a parent. These considerations led me the problematisation of fatherhood and fathers' discourse. I argued for a radical separation of the understanding of fatherhood from biological considerations and a more contextual anchoring of the concept.

In the next chapter I shall take the notion of contextualisation of gender and men's discourse further. I shall show that the men construct themselves in such apparently masculine spheres as work and 'bread-winning' similarly to women and explore the notion of constructing emotions without recourse to either emotive language or emotion labels.

Note

1. The motif of the intactness of children's bedrooms in men's narratives was confirmed ethnographically in a research done by Clare Holdsworth and David Morgan, who found several instances of such stories (personal communication with David Morgan, 22 December 2003).

6
Speaking Helplessly: The Emotions of Unemployment

Men and unemployment

In a piece of research on experiences of unemployment in post-Communist Poland,[1] one of the interviewed men said the following.

Extract 1
RC, male, born 1957, Opole, Poland

> I: what do you feel now as an unemployed person?
>
> RC: well I feel a kind of helplessness that (.) I still have a kind of commitments like alimental, among others, and I am not able, say, to fulfil such commitments and I feel a kind of, as they say, helplessness.

Two aspects of this extract struck me. First, it was the directness of the admission of helplessness, as direct as the ascription of weakness in the first extract of Chapter 2, where a woman in very strong terms decided men were just about useless as regards coping with adversities in life. Second, I was struck by a very particular expression of emotional experience. Helplessness does not normally feature in vocabularies of emotions, but I think there is little doubt that RC is talking about his emotional experience. Even more importantly, however, RC's utterance is putting a label on a more general pattern in the narratives of the unemployed men (and indeed, women) interviewed. It labels constructions of emotional experience, or helplessness, to be exact, without recourse to emotional or emotive language.

In this chapter, I am going to explore the emotional experience of men talking about their unemployment. To a considerable extent this will be the experience of weakness, of sadness, but also the experience of helplessness. Thus I shall discuss parts of the narratives in which men give explicit accounts of their emotions and then I shall explore narratives in which emotional experience is constructed implicitly. Before that it is necessary, I think, to sketch out the social and political context in which to see the data, so I shall say a few words first about the relationship between unemployment and masculinity, and second, about the macro social-political context of Poland where the data were collected.

Using data in Polish in this chapter has two consequences for the discussion in this book. Despite a clear patriarchal underpinning of the Polish dominant model of masculinity (see, e.g., Melosik, 1996, 2002), I am not proposing that the narratives I am going to analyse here parallel or complement those found in the data collected in the UK. I am not claiming that either men's or women's narratives in the UK corpus would display similar characteristics to those here. However, discussing certain linguistic features of narratives in this chapter, I shall be making claims with regard to the construction of 'emotions' rather than Polish or any other emotions. I doubt very much that the 'non-emotive' constructions of emotions is a characteristic of Polish only (indeed, I have already indicated the phenomenon in the previous chapter, using the English data), but yet I cannot make a claim as to the universalness of the phenomenon.

'Stiffed'

In her account of modern masculinity, a radical feminist author proposes a view much sympathetic to men. Men have been stiffed because society has removed the very plank upon which masculinity has hinged: employment. Comparing women's 'problem-with-no-name' (Faludi, 2000:15) with men's predicament, she suggests that while women organised themselves, men, because of the 'master of the universe' kind of masculinity, grow more and more isolated.

Academics are pretty much in agreement. Unemployment is a major assault on one of the foundations of men's identities or masculinity in general (Brittan 1989; Morgan, 1992; Willott and Griffin, 1996, 1997; Willis, 2000). Masculinity has always been associated with paid employment; a man is supposed to provide for himself and his family (Mattinson, 1988); in fact providing for the family is part of the measure of success of what it is to be a man (Hood, 1986; Nonn, 2001; see also contributions to Hood, 1993). Unemployed men feel disempowered, useless, emasculated; their self-esteem is shattered (Brittan, 1989; Beynon, 2002), with the ultimate humiliation constituted by being supported by one's wife (Kelvin and Jarrett, 1985).

Willott and Griffin (1997) offer ethnographic evidence regarding Brittan's (1989) claim that unemployed men need to come to terms with their uselessness. In their study of working-class masculinities they show the unemployed's discourse as constructing them as 'idle scroungers', falling back on the welfare system, rather than paying their way. Unemployed men in that study are consumers who cannot consume (particularly beer at the pub). They are bread-winners without the bread (see also contributions to Gaillie, Marsh and Vogler, 1994). But unemployment is not only about masculinity for masculinity's sake. Unemployed men need to deal also with masculinity in relation to their partners or wives. Willis (2000) proposes that unemployment means shedding the traditional dignity invested in masculinity on account of having a job. This, continues Willis, might have dramatic consequences for working-class women who might be asked to respect the man for what he is, rather than for what he does. And the men will continue working on their biceps' contours and the visibility of their six-packs (Willis, 2000:93). There is also the reverse side of the gender relations coin. Pyke (1996) shows that the masculine power of the 'unsuccessful' man may shift to the resentful wife, since men earning less, let alone the unemployed, can very easily be blamed for not caring enough. This is true in the case of the Mr Phillips character from John Lanchester's novel, *Mr Phillips*: having lost his job, Mr Phillips still keeps up the appearances, gets up, dresses and leaves for work (just like another character in the hugely popular British film *The Full Monty*). How can a man tell his wife that he is not working? Be that as it may, Jones (1991) proposes that it is men's joblessness, rather than being in employment, which challenges the structure of family relationships.

These ideas about unemployment have been encapsulated by a quote from a memoir of an unemployed man cited by one of the leading Polish political weeklies. The 45-year-old unemployed father of six children (who, incidentally, found a job because of the memoir), says:

I cringe when I see the way Masia [wife] looks at a nice piece of clothing or cosmetics for herself. A moment of pensiveness, sometimes a touch, and then a rapid push of the goods away, with a sad smile. And she always hides in me, so we go away. After all, she is a woman, and has a natural need to dress or smell nicely. And it gets me then, because it is I who should buy it for her. I am her husband and I cannot take decent care of her. We both have not bought a single piece of clothing for years. First, you have to take care of the boots, clothing and school items for the children...

When you are unemployed, you dream of blackness. Not a coffee, a woman, just blackness. You wake up at 5 in the morning in blackness. I have work now and I still wake up in blackness, because I know this fucking state. I know how it hurts.

(Polityka, issue 11 2003, my translation)

Patriarchal gender relations in the family, represented by positioning of the husband as the physical 'rock' and the carer are, in fact, what makes this fragment particularly poignant. It is precisely the identity of the 'master of the universe', as Faludi (2000) calls it, that it is the man's undoing. He constructs himself not only as a man, but also as one who cannot fulfil the expectations which society places on him as a man. But the author of the memoir goes on to say that unemployment is not merely a 'legal' condition defined by an employment contract; it goes further than that because unemployment is a lifestyle, or perhaps a lifestyle of having no lifestyle. It is also a stigma, an identity which is not easy to shed (on lived definitions of unemployment, see Kozłowska, 2004).

Post-Communism

Following the policies of *perestroika* and *glasnost* started by Gorbachev in the Soviet Union in mid-1980s, in 1989 the countries of Eastern Europe started undergoing dramatic political and social changes. These changes saw not only a shift from conflictual and oppositional construction of nationhood against other countries to ones focused upon collaboration and unification, but also, importantly, a significant change in internal public discourses. The political transformations of the late 1980s and the beginning of the 1990s were also seen in the increase of public and private liberties for the citizens of Czechoslovakia, Germany and Poland, and in the countries' political alliances.

Since these events the comfortable political certainties and official ideologies of the Cold War have been called into question on both sides of the former Iron Curtain. The introduction of liberalised ideologies, both at the official level and in most of the freed media, also had to be translated into most of the countries' systems. New laws and new textbooks which would accommodate the new social and political realities had to be written. Newly established political parties had to find new ways of communicating with the voters. New official national narratives had to be found.

However, the discursive changes have been coupled with those which, although semiotised and ideologised, can be seen as deep transformations in the social fabric of the communities. State budgets could not cope with just about any significant expenditure, and health and social security systems needed immediate and deep reform. Most importantly, the collapse of heavy nationalised industry meant that jobs were no longer secure and unemployment rose at a frightening rate. The assumptions that these changes have had a significant impact upon people's identities (see, e.g., Marody, 2000) have already been given some empirical grounding, focusing mostly upon public discourses in some of the Eastern European countries (Koczanowicz and Kołodziejska, 1999; Kuzio, 2001). Recently, private discourses have also been given some attention (Meinhof and Galasiński, 2000; Galasińska, Rollo and Meinhof, 2002; Galasiński, 2002; Galasińska 2003).

In this chapter I am focusing on the narratives of those who, to a considerable extent, have lost out due to the transformations. They are people who, for one reason or another, were not able to keep up with changes in the job market. Their stories are those of hardship (sometimes extreme). They are also full of emotion, and this is the dimension I shall explore here.

Emotional unemployment

In this section I shall focus on how the interviewed men talked about unemployment in terms of emotions. I shall show that, despite the supposed standard of controlled 'manly emotions' (Shields, 2002), the speakers talked about emotional extremes. The extremity of the event – losing one's job, or the inability to find one – is associated with an extremity of emotional experience.

Extract 2
PZ, male, born 1949, interviewed in Opole, Poland

I: what did you feel when you learnt about it, about losing your job.

PZ: look miss, I mean, what? Breakdown, innit? So. My wife didn't want to believe at all that I would not have a job. And what? You see I brought [home] my notice. Psychology.

Extract 3
WL, male, born 1960, interviewed in Opole, Poland

I: what do you feel now as an unemployed person?

WL: I mean what do I feel? I am not sinking with it, right? Because I know it has to pass, that something will come up, right? Well, it's obvious that the mood is very bad. I said why, didn't I? But to break down or to hang myself or something like that, it won't cross my mind. I am just looking for [a job], obviously, right?

While PZ claims distanced ownership of his breakdown, signifying presumably a host of very strong emotions, WL talks only about potential emotions. His strategy of denying the strongest of emotions leaves him attributing bad moods to himself. But in this denial one can hear a rebuttal of the implicit suspicion of such emotions. Yes, he feels pretty bad; but he has not lost it, he is still fighting. Indeed, despite situating his predicament as outside his capacity to deal with it ('it will pass, something will come up'), he finishes his turn with an agentive construction of himself seeking employment.

This implicit rebuttal of others' voices can also be seen in WL's irritation with the question about his feelings. The answer is implied to be pretty obvious: what would anyone feel about losing their job? By denying the strongest emotions, the speaker gives a good clue as to what kind of emotions one might expect from someone who has lost a job. But there might be another aspect to the irritated responses of both men. They both admit to strong emotions which imply weakness, perhaps even 'unmanliness'. Especially in a still significantly patriarchal Polish society, the model of a man who is not the bread-winner, who is 'reduced' to the role of the house-husband, is definitely not within the repertoire of discourses socially available to men to construct their identities with. Indeed in research on men bringing significantly less income to the household than their wives, Ryba (2003) observes that the interviewed men constructed the situation as something abnormal, which they hope will soon pass. Their wives' ability to earn, moreover, was positioned as an accident, sheer luck rather than a well-deserved outcome of a successful career.

In the next extract, the speaker not only seconds WL in talking about the most severe of emotions, but in fact faces espousing it.

Extract 4
RC, male, born 1957, interviewed in Opole, Poland

I: how do you imagine your future.

RC: I mean how I imagine the future. well, I can see two scenarios. First is that I shall eventually take up employment which will simply enable me, not only me, but also, say, my family, some kind of functioning. Moderately normal. And the other, well I am still on benefit right now and, I qualify. after a time, well, what's left is black despair after losing the right to benefit. Well, it's difficult to live on, say, [my] pensioner mother, isn't it? So the other is rather I don't know (a little) macabre.

Czarna rozpacz (literally 'black despair'), a saying reminiscent of such other Polish phraseologies as *czarna otchłań* ('black abyss'), positions the speaker at the extreme end of the emotional spectrum. There is no stronger despair than that. It seems that the less preferred scenario for the speaker is equated with emotions at the limits of their strength, the weakness reaching breaking point. Is that man still a man? The extract sets out two linguistic scenarios. It is quite fascinating that the scenario of employment is rendered in linguistically agentive terms, while the scenario of unemployment is conveyed in linguistically passive terms. Thus, the first possibility is that the speaker will – actively – take up employment. This action will be enabling insofar as his and his family's lives go. But when he switches to talking about the scenario of losing benefit and not finding employment, the agentivity vanishes. He is talking about 'being' on benefit, 'having' a right to it. The Polish form the speaker uses (*przysługuje mi*, a form which is untranslatable into English; the closest equivalent would be rendering it as 'it applies to me') renders him the linguistic object of the benefit's action. Even the emotions are simply left there for him. Interestingly, the potentially active form of losing benefit which both in Polish and English could be rendered in a linguistically active way ('I lost the benefit'), is nominalised (i.e., an action is rendered as a thing, a verb turned into a noun) into a loss. RC does not claim agentivity even in losing his unemployment benefit.

I argued elsewhere that such discourse of helplessness or disempowerment is characteristic of post-Communist Poland (Galasiński, 2002) and can be seen as constitutive of what I call 'post-Communist' identity. Linguistically people construct their lives as outside their control, lives 'living themselves', so to speak (cf. Polish *żyje się*; see also Ryba, 2003). Incidentally, in extract 3, WL also positions the change of his situation and new employment opportunities as occurring of their own accord, without his intervention.

Helplessness

Helplessness does not need to be associated with the linguistic passive voice, however, or the positioning of the speakers as objects, mere recipients of others' actions. I think helplessness is a broader notion and I would like to explore it in this chapter as a means of constructing emotional experience. On a theoretical level, what I am proposing is that speakers can construct their emotions without availing themselves of the emotional potential of language: either of the so-called emotive language (Ochs and Schieffelin, 1989; Caffi and Janney, 1994), or the vocabulary which labels emotional experience (Bellelli, 1995). The last point in particular needs some elaboration. So far, I have been basing my analysis upon two kinds of utterances. The first kind were those utterances in which speakers explicitly named their emotions, using (for example) labels of emotions, such as *love, worry, hate* and *fear*. This is the most clear and unambiguous of evidence. Alternatively, I was proposing that speakers' references to 'traumatic experiences', or to children being important, refer also to emotional experience, albeit indirectly. Such expressions are taken to imply emotional experience on the basis of our abilities as social actors to interpret the world. We all know that if someone is talking about the importance of their children, he or she is referring to love, empathy, worry for them. But, this time, I would like to argue that emotional experience can be constructed in terms other than the two kinds I have just mentioned. I shall argue that other lexico-grammatical resources of language can also construct emotional experience without labelling it, without even implying it by certain, should I say, 'key' vocabulary. Incidentally, this vocabulary, or indeed one labelling emotions in general, is far from obvious. As Fiehler (2002) observes, the language used to describe our 'internal' feelings is also used with cognitive, motivational or physiological meanings.

The possibility of a language of emotions without explicit references to emotionality has of course been argued. There are a number of scholars who see the 'language of emotions' not only in terms of emotion labels, but also in such terms as metaphors, idioms, emotional verbs, stylisations and others (see Foolen, 1997; Fiehler, 2002). Shimanoff (1985), in her study of how people talked about their emotions, proposed also to take on board expressions from which one can infer an internal state as I did in my second strategy. Thus she classified utterances such as 'It drives him up the wall' as a reference to emotions. Greenwood (1994), however, goes the furthest in his conception of the 'language of emotions'. Although his argument concerned primarily the extent to which labelling of emotions constitutes them (which is largely irrelevant here), Greenwood proposes, importantly, that 'the only "language of emotions" necessary for emotional experiences is the language of moral commentary on actions and social relations' (Greenwood, 1994:165–6). He continues by saying that emotions evolve in particular forms of social life, which I take to refer to discourse as a particular set of social practices constitutive of social life. Greenwood does not put his claim to empirical test, though. How exactly one can construct emotional experience without using explicit or implicit, more or less fixed, linguistic expressions will be what I would like to explore below.

I would like to stress again the distinction between 'doing an emotion' in discourse, here and now, and an account of emotion, here and now. Both construct emotions but, while the former constructs also an emotional person, the other does not. These constructions also differ in the resources they are likely to utilise. In order to 'do an emotion', here and now, one does not have to use (but of course one might) emotional labels or other linguistic resources which implicitly or explicitly describe emotions. One does not need to say one is angry to perform anger. One will presumably use emotive language with a number of other paralinguistic features that will be conventionally associated with anger (see, e.g., Planalp, 1999). In contrast, accounts of anger do not have to (although clearly might) construct an angry person, here and now. You do not need to be angry in order to tell a story of your anger. This is where one might use emotional labels, metaphors or references to traumatic experiences. Some of these resources will of course overlap with those used by people who do 'do' emotion here and now. Here I am interested only in accounts and the way they are put together. My argument in turn here is that, in contrast to most research I know of, an account of emotional experience does not need to use the language explicitly or implicitly associated with it, whether emotional labels or other such expressions.

Now, I think one can define helplessness in terms similar to the definition of frustration offered by Wierzbicka (1999). The core of Wierzbicka's definition of frustration consists of the statement: 'I wanted to do something now, I thought I could do it now, I see (have to think) that I can't do it' (Wierzbicka, 1999:72). The difference one would introduce to this kind of definition is an element indicating the finality of the situation (perhaps something like to 'nothing can be done about it'), together with the presentness of the situation (thus 'I want to do something', perhaps also 'I want something to happen'). One might also consider the introduction of the element of hopelessness into the concept. Thus if Wierzbicka defines hope as 'I don't know what will happen, some good things can happen (some time after now), I want these things to happen' (Wierzbicka, 1999:59), hopelessness could be defined as the opposite, something like: 'I think no good things can happen.' Such an element would introduce a dimension of the feeling of the impossibility of change which, I think, is present in the concept of helplessness. I have some reservations in that while rendering my views on the concepts at hand, these formulations are only tentative indications rather than a formal description of emotional concepts the way Wierzbicka intends. Interestingly, one of the unemployed informants offered a 'lived' account of helplessness which can be found in extract 5. A note on the translation is necessary. NN uses the Polish adjective *bezradny*, rather than *bezsilny* (as RC in extract 1). These are both normally rendered as 'helpless', although their meanings differ slightly: the former is more 'one who does not cope', while the other is closer to 'one who is powerless'.

Extract 5
NN, male, born 1948, interviewed in Opole, Poland

> NN: They teach you over there [at university], put in your head and so on and it's a different world there. You graduate from university, and go out to this shit, because it's a gutter, pure gutter, that's all. And here it turns out you are helpless.
>
> I: mmm.
>
> NN: that what they taught you, you can [shove], your filled note books, books, you can keep it for yourself as a curiosity. This diploma and so on. You decide nothing, you can do nothing.
>
> I: mmm.
>
> NN: nothing. You are simply an instrument. You are an instrument. You could say, understand this some time ago, when the Communists [lit. commune] put the brakes on any initiative and so on. And so on.
>
> I: mmm
>
> NN: put the brakes on initiative and suppressed, as it you used to be said, when a nail stuck out of the plank, on its head. Hammer it right in. into the line, equally with the comrades.
>
> I: mmm.
>
> NN: in my case right? That's the way it was. All the time it was like that. Because I used to have initiative, ideas and so on. But how, if not a comrade had initiative, it was unimportant. Hammer him in.
>
> I: mmm.
>
> I: but now you also had initiative.

NN: now they had initiative and so on and nothing. Because the set-up is still red. Fucking set-up stayed on. I could mention whole firms where the same family works. So on the one hand it is said, it is said, initiative and so on, do, open firms, small, and so on

I: and on the other everything must be the way they want.

NN: and all this no it's unbelievable, one nightmare, this is just one nightmare. So how can you live in this nightmare? You can live. But how? How?

This account is probably as much one of helplessness as it is of the situation of post-Communist Poland in which helplessness is the order of the day, with university studies being of little help in taking control of one's initiative, one's life. The helplessness here is more than an individual emotion, a feeling: it is also a condition of life of a society (on emotions on a societal level, see De Rivera, 1992). This is the way the system makes you be. It results in one not having control over one's life, except that here it is more about being an instrument in someone else's hands, the 'someone' never being identified. The final question 'how to live?' resembles JW's questions in extract 6. So what I am going to argue here is that it is the linguistic structure, anchored within a particular social and cultural context, that constructs helplessness. In other words, it is not merely a content category: it is also a category of form. Here is the first extract to illustrate this point.

Extract 6
JW, male, born 1957, interviewed in Opole, Poland

I: and what do you now feel as an unemployed person.

JW1: I have some neurosis I am getting. I am ill, everything hurts.

I: your body hurts? Or do you mean it hurts like

JW2: The body too. (as if) I was doing something. I walk round the flat, to and fro. I don't know which way to turn. Where to go? Well, where shall I go? Especially that now that it's summer so perhaps I shall find somewhere on a building site or something. because in winter, I happened on the winter period.

I: because it has been since September, hasn't it?

JW3: Right, in the winter period. Since September, I still got my pay in September, because for August right? So it was still, but then it was already November, December and it ended and now it's March, the end, April. And I went like madness, I simply did not know what to do with myself, either. And I tried not to think. Because I say what's going to be tomorrow, what's going to be tomorrow? There is still money for now, what's going to be later? And when I lie down or sit down and think of nothing and when I think to myself I am literally getting hot. I am literally getting hot. I would have a taste for drinking something, getting drunk, let alone smoke a cigarette, right? So I'll take and drink two three coffees, even four coffees a day. Because of the nerves. When I did, I used to drink only at work, they made it [coffee] for 6 [o'clock], and later at 12, if I felt like it or didn't. when it was hot who wanted to drink hot coffee? And in winter a second coffee, and now I'll drink three before 11. Because I am restless [lit. something carries me]. Literally restless [lit. something carries me]. I'll take a (crossword), but how much can you do that? You know. till 11, from 8 before 11 I'll drink three coffees. I have already drunk two today, I'll go home I'll drink more, or some time in the afternoon, and where is 5 o'clock? But I simply miss something, I am restless [lit. something carries me], I simply don't know what to do with myself. I am simply restless [lit. something carries me] . . .

JW4: I still pray that I can arrange for a job somewhere and work a bit more, I don't know what will happen later. First the thought all the time about, to find a job, any job, just find. It makes no difference what I'll do. Because it makes no sense any more. It's better to do something than sit at home. Because at home, what at home? Nerves and nerves and I guzzle this coffee [augmentative] after coffee [augmentative]. Because it makes no difference any more.

JW shows himself to be pretty desperate after losing his job, his desperation constructed also in terms of somatic symptoms which, interestingly, are taken at face value by the interviewer, rather than metaphorically. The Polish *wszystko mnie boli* ('everything hurts') is rarely meant literally, but rather indicates a general poor condition, physical and/or psychological. The only time he picks up the notion of physicality of his emotional turmoil is when he says that he is getting hot when thinking about his situation. Both elements of the story suggest the great, perhaps even extreme, strength of the speaker's feelings, but most of the narrative does not pick up on it explicitly, continuing the story about the speaker's daily life. This story, I think, is about feeling helpless.

What is most striking about JW's narrative is both the construction of the lack of purpose, lack of direction in the informant's life (the informant actually asks the question himself, saying 'which way to turn?'). Let me first focus upon the choice of verbs which the informant uses. In JW2 there are four verbs of movement: *obrócić*, 'turn'; *chodzić* 'walk'; but also *iść* and *pojść* (both translatable as 'go' with implication of going on foot). Interestingly, only *chodzić* is used in an agentive structure with the speaker as the actor. But the Polish *chodzić*, as an iterative verb, also suggests lack of destination. In fact, the speaker explicitly connects *chodzić* with lack of direction, as he walks round the flat. The verbs which do imply direction or destination are used in questions of, significantly, direction. Such use of *chodzić* is repeated in JW3 where the informant constructs himself as walking like madness. The lack of direction in movement is also underscored in his repeated construction of his restlessness. In contrast to the English form, the Polish one (*Nosi mnie*, which I translated as 'I am restless') is conveyed by an actorless verb, the object of which is the speaker. He is being carried, thus positioned in the role of the patient, the object of someone or something else's actions. The directionless speaker's life is also constructed by the rhetorical questions he asks; these are questions for which there is no hint of an answer. The first two questions in JW2, as I have already noted, explicitly ask about where the speaker might want to go. And even though these questions follow from the speaker's words about spending his days walking round his flat, there is little doubt they can also be seen as asking about how to engage with life outside. The next two questions in JW3 show his uncertainty even better. The lack of direction is reinforced by the uncertainty of the future, especially given constructions of time as directional in modern European cultures.

The lack of purpose in life, however, is also constructed in the part of the narrative which I see as being particularly poignant and crucial to the construction of helplessness: the informant's account of drinking coffee. We see someone who is positioning himself in a sort of vicious circle of senseless activities from which there is no escape. Moreover, the informant juxtaposes his current coffee drinking practices with those of the time in employment. He not only drank less coffee at work but, more importantly, the drinking practices at work were much more ordered. It was not only about drinking coffee, it was also about the structure of the day. It all seems to have collapsed now. Now he simply drinks coffee without any order or pattern. The adverb *nawet* ('even', as in 'even four coffees'), referring to the amount of coffee drunk, shows the uncontrollability (and compulsiveness) of the practice. Note also that the current coffee drinking is not something done in its own right: it is a substitute for drinking alcohol, or for smoking a cigarette. Moreover, in the context of work, the speaker shows it as a choice because in summer one might, but might not, have the coffee. This is immediately followed by the irritated 'and now I'll drink three before 11'. Importantly, the Polish original contains as many as two explicit references to himself, using the pronoun *ja* ('I') in its linguistic form. Such a form is marked in that in Polish the form of the verb also carries information about the grammatical person. In other words, one does not need to say *ja* ('I') in order to indicate that one is referring to oneself.

The senselessness of drinking coffee is complemented by its compulsiveness which is rendered by the verb forms. Despite the fact that the informant speaks of his daily practices, he does not use the iterative forms of the verbs (something that would be rendered in English by the present tense, as in 'I drink', 'I take', etc.). Rather, he chooses perfective words in the present tense, thus indicating activity which has been completed. Normally in Polish, perfective verbs in the present tense serve to refer to the future; they can, however, as in this particular context, indicate a certain irritating compulsiveness of the activity. Incidentally, the compulsiveness of drinking coffee is reinforced by its being directly linked to the informant's nerves. The reference to the time of the day, once again by a rhetorical question ('where is 5 o'clock?'), is a final reinforcement of the speaker's construction of the new habit as senseless, compulsive. I think the kind of imagery this extract creates is that of an animal in a cage pining to get out, but the confines do not allow it. The informant (right from the initial reference to walking round the flat) constructs himself as confined to it, on his own, trying to kill time, unable to do anything about the situation. But there is no aggression in what he says. His walking round the flat is not like the pacing of an angry animal, ready to jump at any moment; this is an image of someone who has already been taken over by the situation, or perhaps by the coffee.

The second fragment of extract 6 makes some of the constructions more explicit. In JW4 the informant explicitly talks about the senselessness of the situation, surrendering to it and giving up all expectations of employment. But this time he also positions himself as an agent. What is quite fascinating here is that the only time he constructs himself as an unfettered agent is when he refers to his prayers. Prayer is the last resort: this is just about the last thing he does of his own accord (note the use of 'still'). And it is through prayer – an action of saying things – that he constructs his potential agency of arranging for a job and work, both rendered as infinitives. But even this potential agency is undermined by 'a bit more'. His expectations reach rock bottom in another expression of potential agency: 'It makes no difference what I'll do'. Finally, even when he drinks coffee, he stops being an agent in his own right. The reference to 'guzzling' (Polish *żłopać*, an augmentative of 'drink') and to *kawsko* (augmentative of *kawa* 'coffee') indicates his irritation with the activity. He does not like what he does, so this is once again an implicit reference to compulsion.

This is a story of someone who has been taken over by the situation, who has lost his direction in life, someone helpless. It is rendered not only by the content of what he says; more importantly, helplessness is constructed by the lexico-grammatical resources of language. It is interesting to note that JW's construction of himself being locked out of the world is not unique: we can also see it in the next extract in which the speaker positions himself as being lonely in his flat.

Extract 7
PZ, male, born 1949, interviewed in Opole, Poland

I: when you get up, what do you do?

PZ: I make breakfast for the boy and see him out for his placement and go to buy a newspaper. I clean the house, vacuum, make beds. This is my work [job].

I: and what next?

PZ: I sit at home like a hermit and look out of the window. Because how much can you walk? When someone tells me once I have no job for you. So what for?

I: mmm.

PZ: you see yourself that in the newspaper now, only 30, 35, tops.

The somewhat irritated reference to housework as 'his work', in which we can probably hear the masculine stereotype of housework as unmanly, is followed by the explicit reference to being a hermit. Despite the activeness of the linguistic form – the speaker is actively engaged in sitting and looking – it is also motionless. One could probably see it as being complementary to JW's narrative in which the verbs of motion were put in rhetorical questions, with the agency put in question. Here the agency is explicit, yet the verbs imply stasis.

A comment on the practice of looking out of the window of flats in tenement houses is necessary here. Particularly in working-class areas in Polish towns and cities, one can occasionally see elderly people who spend their days looking out of the window, watching the life of their neighbours and of the street. The flat's window is almost the only window to the world, with the people looking being either physically or psychologically unable to leave the flat. Speaking of himself as looking out of the window the speaker not only writes himself into the practice, but also positions himself as part of the group of people sitting in the windows doing absolutely nothing all day. One can hear the resignation in his words. He is just about only good for sitting in the window and doing nothing.

PZ's helplessness is accounted for, however. It is not as if he does not want to look for a job. It is more about other people, those who told him they had no job for him, so there is no point in asking again. Moreover, it is also about his age: job adverts look for people who are at most 35 years of age. However, I do not think this account is given with the aim of justifying sitting at home. The negativity of the description, being a hermit or looking out of the window, is too strong for the latter part of the extract to give the speaker the licence just to sit at home. I think that as much as we probably see the implicit reference to the stereotype of masculinity in his first move, the latter account is designed to be face-saving. The speaker does not want to appear to be just a window-looker to the interviewer (a young woman); there are reasons why it happens and they are nothing to do with him.

The final extract in this section is similar in constructing helplessness, lack of direction in life, its complete uncertainty.

Extract 8
WL, male, born 1960, interviewed in Opole, Poland

> WL: So that's why I come here, because I come often and I seek [a job]. Perhaps something can be found that will suit me and will suit this company where I will fit in, right? And I come with positive thinking that surely there will be something like that, right? Because they change, there is movement in companies all the time, some retire, go on sickness benefit or something or other. Obviously something is freed up all the time, isn't it? And so the company is reasonable and so you can survive, right? So one can know that this tomorrow is somehow assured, that you sleep, in the morning you know that you go to work and that everything is all right, and not that you sleep and you go to bed and you don't know what to do with yourself the following day. What to do, what to cook in the pot and so on. And what to buy it with. So.

The glimmer of hope, stressed so hard by the speaker in his reference to his positive thinking, is followed by the construction of life as something dramatically uncertain. This uncertainty is not merely that of finding employment, it is much more basic: the ability to sleep, to have food and the means to buy it. Note again the contrast between the hypothetical active 'going to work' and passive 'what to do with oneself'. The passiveness can also be seen at the beginning of the extract in the statement of hope. Also here the speaker is not positioning himself as actively looking for a job, or a company he would like to work for. Rather, the use of *pasować* ('fit in') positions him as a piece of a jigsaw puzzle. The informant does not even attribute finding a job to himself (Polish *znajdzie się* has the verb used in a reflexive voice and can best be translated as 'find itself'). Finally, the success of finding a position is measured by survival, a reference to a living with one's basic needs catered for. But, again, it is not the informant who earns his half-decent living, it is the company that lets him have it.

What I have been arguing in this section is that the experience of helplessness does not have to be narrated by an explicit reference to an inability to succeed, but can also be shown by the linguistic form of the utterance. I would like to suggest more generally that emotions are not merely constructed by the content of what is said, by the so-called emotive language, or explicit references to emotional experience, but also by the lexico-grammatical resources of language.

Gendered helplessness?

Now, helplessness, weakness, as I said a number of times, is stereotypically associated with femininity. Men don't cry. Men are supposed to be strong, to cope, to offer a helping hand to women. In the narratives I presented in the previous sections, men are anything but. They both explicitly and implicitly position themselves as people who have no control over their lives, who walk around senselessly. But the question I want to ask in this section is whether there is anything particularly masculine about their helplessness? Are women helpless in a different way? In other words, is helplessness gendered? Have a look at the following extracts in which unemployed women construct helplessness.

Extract 9
DS, female, born 1953, interviewed in Opole, Poland

I: and how do you explain your lack of success in finding work?

DS: lack of success? I mean in that there are very few vacancies for one. Those who want to take on somebody, who advertise they make selections. They simply classify people. And I think that if someone is younger, right? Then they will get on faster than me, right? So. I suspect that because that's my experience. That it was like that.

I: and how do you imagine your future?

DS: future? well, here it's like that if one had some cash, money, one could perhaps manage in life because one could think of something. And if you are poor all the time, and the situation here will not change, I will I think be only at the mercy of my children. As long as these children have some these material conditions better, right? So I think, because now I suspect my children might lose their jobs . . .

DS: you see only now I can see it in this questionnaire.[2] Because really if I had such qualifications, right? Also computers or something, I am for this computer, I would have to in glasses. Because I have [laughs] my age, right? Even if I did train in computers who would take me on? Everyone prefers in some company to get someone younger, right? For something like that because now they need a lot of people for trade, for computers, right? But you have to have skills in cashiers and the like. So. I would have to myself. What would it benefit me if I took private tuition, such training and then they would not take me on, because they will say she is too old.

The first aspect of DS's accounts I would like to draw attention to is the constructed impossibility of getting a job. Employers want other people, younger people (a trait also found in men's narratives). Linguistically, it is the employers, the 'they', people in power (see also Galasińska, 2003) who are positioned as actors. In the first fragment, she is only an agent in mental clauses: she thinks, while they make their selections. The constructions are made explicit in her reference to being at the mercy of the children (an expression associated with begging, lower status, ultimate powerlessness). In the second fragment, the informant positions herself as an actor, yet in conditional clauses. She would do things – train, work with computers, have skills – but all these potentially active clauses are disavowed by another reference to the 'they' who have the power to declare her unfit for work, because she is too old. There is no point in doing anything. The speaker's agency is immediately undermined. This extract could easily be used in tandem with the narratives offered by men: there are similar themes, similar linguistic constructions, perhaps even similar helplessness. It seems that there is very little evidence that helplessness is gendered.

If anything, in fact, one might want to argue that if helplessness is gendered, it is perhaps the domain of men; women's narratives could in fact be seen as less helpless. One of the female informants, when asked about what she felt when she was told about losing her job, said that she did not feel anything and offered an economic explanation as to why companies made redundancies. The following extract presents her answer to the question of what she felt as an unemployed person. The rationality and positiveness of this last extract, its strength, if you like, cannot be found among the men's narratives.

Extract 10
KJ, female, born 1960, interviewed in Opole, Poland

KJ: well, I can still seek [employment] for another 3 months, half a year. But then I shall have to, here I thought of this kind, while doing work at home,[3] I shall be phoning other provinces, other [jobseekers'] centres. But this is more difficult as it would mean changing the place of living. But I would be prepared to change the place of living if I managed to get a job and make sure of having a reasonable place to live. Because going away means living somewhere. But I am able to change the city, place of living if it meant securing employment.

Most of KJ's answers are similar. If she cannot get employment to suit her qualifications, she will look for something requiring lower skills. Failing that, she will look for something else. Then she will look somewhere else. Every time it is like a plan, a positive way forward. It is always active, and never involves walking round the flat senselessly waiting for the job to find itself (see also Kitzinger's (2000) account of women as active agents in the social world). But is this activeness something to do with her being a woman? Or perhaps she is performing masculinity? Or is it perhaps to do with the fact that she is a qualified accountant, a professional whose skills are in some moderate demand in Poland? And that work is important in her life.

Conclusions

I had two main objectives in this chapter. First I wanted, once again, to demonstrate that men can and do show their experience in terms of their emotions. This time, perhaps because of the nature of the experience, they did it in terms of extreme emotions. There was hardly any attempt to show control of emotions, as cultural models of masculinity or emotions might predict. Unemployment took over.

The second objective of the chapter was to argue that emotions, 'helplessness' in the case discussed in this chapter, do not have to be constructed in terms of vocabulary which in one way or another implies emotional experience. What I tried to show was that other lexico-grammatical resources of language, typically not associated with emotional experience, can also construct it. Speakers did not need either to label the experience or to describe themselves as unable to do things.

Finally, I argued that, as with parenthood in the last chapter, helplessness seems to be gender free. Women's accounts of helplessness were clearly very similar to men's, except that, in some accounts of activity, hopes of getting a job were expressed by women rather than men. The question of the extent to which such accounts are to do with gender will be tackled in the final chapter of the book.

Appendix: original versions of Polish extracts

Extract 1

I: a co pan teraz czuje jako osoba bezrobotna?

RC: no ja czuję no taką pewnego rodzaju bezsilność że (.) yyy mam pewnego rodzaju jeszcze zobowiązania załóżmy no yyy alimentacyjne między innymi również i nie jestem w stanie powiedzmy wypełniać takich zobowiązań i no czuję pewnego rodzaju jak to mówią bezsilność.

Extract 2

I: co pan czuł jak się dowiedział o tym o: utracie pracy?

PZ: pani, no no no co? no załamanie nie? no. (. .) żona to nie chciała w ogóle w to wierzyć że ja tam nie będę y: miał pracy. i co? ale widzi pani, no przyniosłem zwolnienie (. .) psychika.

Extract 3

I: y: co pan czuje obecnie jako osoba bezrobotna?

WL: to znaczy co ja czuje no h(h)h. ja: tam nie pogrążam się z tym nie? bo wiem że to: musi minąć, że w końcu coś się znajdzie nie? no wiadomo że: samopoczucie jest bardzo złe nie? no mówiłem dlaczego nie? ale no żeby się załamywać żeby się wieszać czy coś w tym rodzaju to ani mi do głowy nie przyjdzie nie? po prostu szukam bo to wiadomo nie?

Extract 4

I: jak pan wyobraża sobie swoją przyszłość?

RC: (.) znaczy no że jak wyobrażam sobie przyszłość. no jawią mi się powiedzmy dwa scenariusze jakieś. pierwszy to takie że w końcu podejmę jakieś zatrudnienie które no po prostu umożliwi mi nie tylko mi ale i powiedzmy mojej rodzinie jakieś funkcjonowanie. w miarę normalne. a drugi no to że po prostu no w tej chwili jestem na jeszcze na zasiłku, przysługuje mi po pewnym czasie no to: pozostaje nie wiem no czarna rozpacz po po utracie już prawa do zasiłku no po prostu nie wiem, no trudno być na utrzymaniu powiedzmy mamy emerytki prawda bo. także ten drugi to jest raczej taki no nie wiem no makabryczny (trochę).

Extract 5

NN: tam panią uczą, kładą pani do głowy i tak dalej i tam jest inny świat pani kończy uczelnie, wychodzi pani do tego gnoju, bo to jest rynsztok to jest czysty rynsztok (.) to wszystko, i tu się okazuje że pani jest bezradna.

I: [uhm uhm

NN: [że pani to co panią uczyli to (.) to może pani sobie y: zapisała pani zeszyty książki to może pani sobie jako ciekawostkę zachować dla siebie. ten dyplom i tak dalej. pani o niczym nie decyduje, pani nic nie może zrobić nic.=

I:=uhm

NN: nic. po prostu jest pani narzędziem. narzędziem pani jest. (..) no to (.) to przecież no: można było kiedyś powiedzieć zrozumieć jak komuna y: hamowała wszelką inicjatywę i tak dalej [i tak dalej.

I: [uhm

NN: hamowała inicjatywę i tłumiła no tak jak się mówiło jak gwóźdź wystawał w desce to go w łeb. i wbić go, [na równo, na równo z towarzyszami.

I: [uhm uhm uhm

NN: w moim przypadku było tak? y: było tak. cały czas tak było. no bo ja byłem z inicjatywą z pomysłami i tak dalej. ale no jak, jak nie towarzysz miał inicjatywę, [to nie ważne. trzeba go wbić.

I: [uhm

I: no ale teraz też miał pan [inicjatywę

NN: [i teraz mieli inicjatywę i tak dalej i tak dalej i nie da. bo układy zostały czerwone. kurewskie układy zostały i y: no już bym nie wymienił te całe biura to sama rodzina pracuje. (..) no. (..) no i cóż. z jednej strony mówi się mówi się inicjatywa i tak dalej, róbcie [otwierajcie firmy, drobne, i tak dalej

I: [a z drugiej strony musi być po ich myśli i=

NN:=a to wszystko nie, no po prostu to jest coś niesamowitego, to jest jeden koszmar, to jest jeden koszmar. to jak w tym koszmarze można żyć. można żyć. no jak? jak?

Extract 6

I: a co pan czuje obecnie jako osoba bezrobotna?

JW: ja mam nerwicę jakąś dostaję. ja chory już jestem, mnie wszystko boli.

I: ale boli ciało? czy boli tak y

JW: y no ciało też. (jakbym) coś robił. chodzę po mieszkaniu tam i z powrotem. nie wiem w którą stronę się obrócić. gdzie iść? no gdzie pójdę? tym bardziej jak teraz lato to może gdzieś znajdę gdzieś na budowie albo coś bo (.) bo w zimie to ja akurat trafiłem na ten okres zimowy taki.

I: no tak bo od września prawda?

JW: no akurat ten okres zimowy. od września jeszcze we wrześniu dostałem wypłatę bo za sierpień nie? no to tak jeszcze tak (.) no a potem już listopad grudzień i się skończyło no i teraz już marzec jest koniec kwiecień. wtedy chodziłem jak obłęd, nie wiedziałem po prostu co ze sobą zrobić też. a starałem się tylko nie myśleć. bo tak mówię co będzie jutro co będzie jutro? na razie jeszcze pieniądze są ale co będzie potem? a tak jak się położę albo jak siądę i o niczym nie myślę to jak mi się to myśli to mi się to mnie się już normalnie gorąco się robi. normalnie mi się gorąco robi. ja już bym miał smaka się napić czego upić się już tam nie mówię że papierosa zapalić, prawda? to też wezmę dwie trzy kawy wypiję, cztery kawy nawet dziennie. z nerwów. jak piłem to tylko w pracy to wypiłem już tam na szóstą sobie zrobili i potem tam o dwunastej jak miałem ochotę czy jak nie miałem ochoty, jak było gorąco to komu się chciało ciepłą kawę nawet pić. a w zimie to tam drugą kawę, a tak to ja teraz ja do jedenastej wypiję trzy. bo mnie nosi. normalnie nosi. (krzyżówkę) wezmę, ile to można pisać tego. no wie pani. do jedenastej, od ósmej do jedenastej wypiję trzy kawy. dzisiaj już wypiłem dwie, przyjadę do domu wypiję jeszcze też, albo gdieś jeszcze po południu, a gdzie jeszcze piąta? ale mi po prostu czegoś brakuje coś mnie nosi, nie wiem co z sobą po prostu zrobić. no nosi po prostu.

JW: [...] ja jeszcze się modlę żeby jakąś robotę gdzieś załatwić i: (.) pracować jeszcze trochę nie wiem jak dalej. najpierw myśl cały czas o (.) znaleźć jakąś robotę, byle jaką ale by znaleźć. już obojętnie co ja będę robił. bo to już jest bez sensu. lepsze to coś robić jak w domu siedzieć. bo w domu co w domu? nerwy i nerwy i żłopię to kawsko za kawskiem. bo już nic nie daje.

Extract 7

I: jak pan wstaje rano to co pan robi?

PZ: no chłopakowi śniadanie szykuję i: (..) odprawię go na praktykę i: (..) po gazetę idę. (.) w domu posprzątam, po- odkurzę, wersalki pościelę. no i to jest moja praca no.

I: i co potem?

PZ: siedzę w domu, jak pustelnik i i przez okno patrzę. no przecież ile to można te chodzić? jak mi ktoś powie raz [nie mam do ciebie roboty. no to po co?

I: [uhm

PZ: a zresztą widzi (..) widzi pani że w gazecie teraz (.) no trzydzieści, trzydzieści pięć to góra. (..)

Extract 8

WL: no. i dlatego przychodzę tutaj bo przychodzę często i szukam. może akurat coś się znajdzie takiego co (.) co mi będzie pasowało i będzie pasowało zakładowi temu gdzie ja będę pasował nie? a w tej dobrej myśli przychodzę że na pewno coś takiego będzie nie? bo to zmieniają się bo to cały czas jest ruch w zakładach pracy to jedni idą na emeryturę na rentę jakieś tam jeszcze jakieś tam inne. no wiadomo że zawsze coś się zwalnia nie? no i zakład żeby w miarę taki jakiś był żeby można było przeżyć nie? żeby wiedzieć że to jutro jest jednak że jakieś *pewne*, że śpisz rano wiesz że idziesz do pracy i że wszystko w porządku, a nie (.) że śpisz i: (..) kładziesz się i nie wiesz co na drugi dzień rano robić ze sobą. co robić i (.) co do garnka wrzucić i tak dalej nie? i za co żeby to kupić. no. (..)

Extract 9

I: a czym pani tłumaczy niepowodzenia w znalezieniu pracy?

DS: niepowodzenia? to znaczy, w tym że: są jest bardzo mało nie tych miejsc wolnych nie, to jest raz. nie. ci co chcą sobie kogoś przyjąć co to ogłaszają no to oni wybierają nie? po prostu segregują sobie tych ludzi. no i wtedy uważam że jak jest ktoś młodszy nie? no to i tak się prędzej ode mnie załapie niż ja nie? no. ja tak przypuszczam że bo tak właśnie takie y doświadczenia już miałam nie? że tak było.

I: jak wyobraża pani sobie swoją przyszłość?

DS: przyszłość? no właśnie to jest u nas jest tak że jak człowiek by miał trochę gotówki pieniędzy, to by jakoś może sobie poradził w życiu bo by coś jeszcze wymyślił nie? a jak się jest cały czas biednym, a się u nas sytuacja nie zmieni to (.) to będę chyba tylko na tym, na na: łasce u dzieci moich. o ile te dzieci też będą miały jakieś te nie? warunki materialne lepsze, nie? tak myślę, bo teraz na przykład przypuszczam że może jak nawet moje dzieci stracą pracę […]

DS: […] o widzi pani bo akurat tutaj dopiero w tej ankiecie to widzę. bo rzeczywiście jak ja bym miała yyy takie kwalifikacje nie? też na ten na komputery albo coś ale ja ja już jestem ten na komputer to ja też bym już w okularach musiała. bo ja już mam [laughs] taki wiek nie? i gdzie by mnie ktoś przyjął? nawet jak bym się wyszkoliła w tym komputerze, nie? to też każdy woli w tam w jakimś zakładzie pracy (.) y załatwić sobie kogoś młodszego, nie? na takie coś, bo teraz dużo osób potrzebują, do handlu na komputer nie? ale to trzeba mieć tą znajomość tych kas i tego nie? no. bym musiała se. a co by mi to dało że ja wezmę sobie prywatnie taką tą takie szkolenie a i tak mnie potem nie przyjmą, bo powiedzą a już za stara. […]

Extract 10

KJ: jeżeli jeszcze no powiedzmy mogę jeszcze trzy miesiące pół roku szukać. (..) ale potem będę musiała się (.) tu myślałam o: tym rodzaju na na następnym przy pracy już chałupniczej będę dzwoniła już po innych województwach po innych urzędach, może ale (.) to to jest już trudniejsza sprawa ponieważ wiązałaby się z: zmianą miejsca zamieszkania. ale byłabym gotowa nawet zmienić miejsce zamieszkania gdyby udało mi się pozyskać pracę i w miarę zapewnić y: jakieś mieszkanie lokal utrzymaniowy bo automatycznie wyjazd wiąże się z: mieszkaniem gdzieś prawda?

na jakiś zasadach ale jestem zdolna również zmienić y: miasto miejsce zamieszkania gdyby to się wiązało z pozyskaniem nowej pracy. (..)

Notes

1. The research was carried out in the Institute of Psychology at the University of Opole in Poland by Olga Kozłowska for her MA dissertation (see Kozłowska, 2004). She interviewed both men and women and asked them about their experiences of unemployment. Part of her research consisted of a qualitative replication of a quantitative questionnaire and a comparison of the two methodologies with regard to the insight into the 'lived experience' they offer. I am greatly indebted to her for making her data available to me.

   All the extracts quoted in this chapter are my translations of Polish originals which can be found in the Appendix above and, unless otherwise stated, were collected by Olga Kozłowska.

2. After the interview the informants were asked to fill in the questionnaire which was replicated in the interview. They were encouraged to 'think aloud' while completing it. This fragment comes from that part of the session.

3. *Praca chałpunicza* refers to work commissioned by someone and carried out at home; normally it consists of unskilled completion of low-technology devices such as ball point pens or such like.

7
Masculinity? What Masculinity?!

Three things about this book

I would like to make one final argument in this chapter. I want to finish this book with a discussion of the relationship between gender and identity, but before I do this, however, I would like to make a brief review of the arguments in the book. It is not so much intended as a thorough review of all the arguments I have made so far, but as a pointer to their most important aspects.

First of all, in this book I set out to take on dominant models of masculinity (and fatherhood), which propose that men – all men, always, universally, and some particular men regularly – are incapable of feeling, expressing or talking about their emotions. I do know men like that, but I also know women like that. I have had conversations with both men and women in which I showed myself as emotional, but I have also had conversations, with both men and women in which I constructed myself as unemotional. It all depended on my conversational goals. The world of such models seems too unproblematic, too broadly swept. Life is more complex than that, and men are more complex than that.

I hope to have shown that evidence against such models is somewhat double-sided. On the one hand, my data showed that the 'lived' model of masculinity – the ways people construct masculinity in their discourse, not prompted by questions about masculinity – does include emotionality. Men are represented as emotional. On the other hand, I also showed that men talk about their emotions, and in a variety of ways, contexts, constructions, presumably depending on who they are, what they want to say, and a host of other reasons that, perhaps, do not concern the fact that they are men at all.

Second, I have offered a problematisation of the 'lived' model of fatherhood, and by extension, I hope, masculinity (a point I shall elaborate on a bit more later). I hope to have dissociated biological fatherhood from 'father-discourse'. In other words, the fact that a biological father speaks about or to his children does not mean that the analyst can assume that it is in the guise of a father that he is speaking. Certain identities, even if easy to point to given the context, need not necessarily be taken: biological fathers could, in fact, be parents. This is my first step towards laying out the 'un-gendered' view of reality I shall develop below.

Third, I would also like to remind readers of my argument that emotions do not need to be constructed with recourse to 'emotion discourse'. In the argument I referred to helplessness, which I took to be an emotion not only because I thought it was an emotion, but because I had data which suggested that people might think of it as an emotion. I hope to have shown that speakers can construct *feeling* helpless by lexico-grammatical resources of language which are not normally associated with emotionality. Although I have not explored the possibility of other emotions being constructed in such a way, I would hypothesise that they can: there is no reason why not, if you like. Such an exploration would, in fact, be an interesting follow-up to this study.

I would like to stress that the book is a not a result of my – however wonderful, systematic and disciplined – thinking about reality and men (or drawing upon my own experience as a man). My arguments are data-driven. I did not need to invent categories or constructions because I had data. There are actually men and women who talk like this. And this point brings me to one last thing I would like to remind readers about. The data showed that the interviewed men speak about emotions in particular ways. When they speak about their relationships, they tend to – it is important to note the non-universalness of practice – distance themselves from the emotions they have. When they speak about their emotions which are targeted at them themselves, they tend to speak of them directly. But there is a fundamental question to be asked here. Are these patterns anything to do with men? Are they to do with masculinity, or perhaps masculinities, or perhaps gender? Do these patterns tell us anything about masculinity? What I would like to explore in the next section is the issue of gender (and particularly masculinity, of course) and its relationship to identities. Are identities necessarily gendered, and is gender omnirelevant in interaction? I could ask, am I always a man?

The question of to what extent the practices of speaking about emotions are to do with masculinity has already been dealt with in

Chapter 1, when I laid down the theoretical basis of this book. I argued that such practices cannot be masculine, as such an assumption would lead to the conclusion that there is some sort of fixed masculinity in the form of discursive practice. I argued that masculinity is either an ideological construct or, alternatively, a locally negotiated identity. Given the variety of the 'language of emotions' used by men, I do not even think that one super-strategy or the other could be associated with masculinity. Even if only men, unlikely as it might be, used distancing strategies in speaking of emotions, the argument would remain the same. It would not change the fact that men also speak of their emotions directly. But, second, even if they did not, gender and masculinity is about local performance, here and now. Such an exclusive use of a discursive strategy would mean that this strategy is particularly conducive to performing masculinity, that it is part of the social construction of how men speak. There is still nothing masculine about the strategy itself.

Gender and identity

Gendering as context-bound

The important and difficult question is to what extent these strategies are in fact used to perform masculine identities. To what extent do men use, say, indirect strategies of speaking about emotions to 'do masculinity'? To what extent are the strategies a pattern of performing masculinity? One could ask this question in a more general way: to what extent are the data I presented about gender? Have I offered any insight into masculine identity? There are, I think, two separate issues which need to be discussed, and they do not necessarily have to be complementary. One issue is that of the analyst's interpretation: her or his claim that in a given context gender was relevant as a category of 'accounting' for what happened. The other issue is whether gender was relevant for the participants such that they, in one way or another, oriented themselves towards it. The two issues are, I think, occasionally presented as one, or at least one is 'displaced' by the other.

Cameron (1998b) provides a very interesting account of gender as an explanatory category. Quoting a husband's question 'Is there any ketchup, Vera?', she argues that while the man had a number of other possibilities in mind when asking the question, it is the assumption about gender roles that means the question is taken by his wife, Vera, as a request to go and fetch the ketchup. Cameron continues by saying that it is for the analyst to establish what kind of gender assumptions are at work in any given interaction. But Cameron is very cautious about pointing out that her interpretation is context-dependent; she never actually makes the point that Vera's husband talks as a man (see also Kiesling, 1997).

While Cameron's point is one of the analyst-perspective, I am not certain it could be easily extended into a 'lived' one. Butler (1990) proposes that gender is not so much about the features of the individual's behaviour as about the socially maintained norms of intelligibility. Ehrlich (2002:745) continues the argument, saying that:

> if gendering is a process by which individuals are made to make cultural sense, it is important to see that this sense-making process is not necessarily grounded exclusively in the talk or behaviour of the individuals being 'gendered'. Rather, such talk or behaviour is contextualised within wider social discourses that make it intelligible or unintelligible, appropriate or inappropriate.

There are two points that might follow from this. It is one thing to argue that what I say might be taken as masculine, as a manly or un-manly way of speaking, that I shall be put into a sex-category and my actions will be judged on the basis of masculine ideologies, but it is quite another thing to say that I necessarily take up a masculine identity because I take up discourses which are associated with it.

As a case in point I would like to offer an example of an interaction quite similar to that of Cameron (1998b). I was once attending a family dinner which was served by an older member of my family, a widow of over 60 years of age, someone close to me. At the table, when the dinner was served by the hostess, I asked, 'Where is the salt?' while at the same time straightening up in my seat, upon which, to my embarrassment, the hostess got up from the table and headed for the kitchen. I started protesting, saying that I was fully capable of going to the kitchen myself, upon which the hostess smiled and said 'Oh well, I am already up anyway.' And she brought the salt.

So what happened? Was the situation gendered? I actually brought this to the dinner conversation, but before I say what was the hostess's account of what happened, I shall offer mine. When I asked the question, I assumed that because of my change of posture, it would be obvious that I was readying myself to get up to go and get the salt. I also assumed that, given that my relationship with the hostess was very close, looking through her kitchen cupboards (I had done so many times before) was perfectly acceptable. But when she got up, I decided immediately that what I had said had been taken as a complaint, and what followed was precisely what Cameron described: the assumptions about gender roles kicked in and the hostess decided that she should serve the man. Given that I knew that her late husband would have expected that, I was quite happy with the interpretation. So I brought it to the conversation and, as delicately as I could, I tried to explain that it is perfectly acceptable for a woman not to interrupt her eating in order to go and get salt for a man at the table. But the problem was that the way the hostess saw what happened had nothing to do with gender. Even though she did notice my physical bid to go and get the salt from the kitchen myself, she decided that explaining where the salt was in the kitchen was considerably more energy-consuming than getting it herself. In other words, going to fetch it was the quickest way of getting the salt on to the table. Her second consideration was something that had not crossed my mind, that one does not permit guests to fetch their own salt from the kitchen. To her, I was also a guest whom she had invited for dinner, and she was playing the good hostess.

Of course, the fact that a social actor rejects a certain interpretation does not necessarily mean that, in analytical terms, it is not a viable one; in other words, even with insight into the post-event conversation, one could still argue about gender assumptions underlying the exchange the way Cameron did: for example, the assumptions of who plays hostess (although the argument in the case of a single person is somewhat problematic). Still, the explanation given to me by my relative seems to be quite reasonable and not easy to reject.

It seems that gendering as a sense-making process, while contextualised in gender ideologies the way Ehrlich proposes, is also contextualised in the actual interaction and could vary according to the participants. I thought what happened was an indication of the assumption of male domination in the society, but my relative thought that it had nothing to do with it. Assuming that this is what happened (and she actually told the truth), we must conclude that gendering does not have to be uniform in the context. More importantly, gendering seems to be local; not just a localised translation of ideologies (as I think Ehrlich suggests) but, rather, a local – and optional – utilisation of such ideologies. This process also assumes the possibility of rejection. Similarly, Edley and Wetherell (1996:110) propose that interaction can in fact offer positions of 'taking the side of the other', to reinterpret one's activities, to reject a particular version of masculinity. Furthermore, such positioning of gender has little relationship, I think, with the performance of gender identities. In my initial move, I was Darek the younger relative; in my accounting of what happened, I was Dariusz Galasiński, an academic. At no time was I performing masculinity. I even think it would be quite difficult to explain the original question in the context of readiness to go and get the salt in terms of gender assumptions.

So what about the postulate of omnirelevance of gender frequently encountered in feminist literature? Well, the analyst might be able to point to the tacit assumptions about gender relations in what people say despite the fact that they might not orient themselves to it, and then the omnirelevance claim is judged case by case on its merits. But there is another understanding of the issue: that gender is omnirelevant as regards people's interactions, that people's interactions are always part of gender work. As Weatherall (2002:779), who first proposes that gender is *potentially* relevant to all interactions (a statement I would agree with), posits a bit later, the challenge of the analysis is 'to demonstrate *how* and *that* participants display their orientation to omnirelevance of gender' (emphasis in original).

In what follows, I shall discuss the issue of performing masculine identities. Are there any markers of masculine identities? Are there any resources which unmistakably link identity construction with masculinity? Related to this is the issue of omnirelevance of gender which I shall explore in the context of identity construction. First, though, I would like to state in more detail my views on identity construction.

Identity

In contrast to folk theories of self and identity (van Langenhove and Harré, 1993), identity is a discursive construct. People do not harbour an inner essence of self which is discovered by the analyst. Identity is a discourse of (not) belonging, similarity and difference, which is continually negotiated and renegotiated within a localised social context. It is therefore a continual process of becoming: always provisional, always subject to change (for an empirically-based discussion of identity construction see Barker and Galasiński, 2001). But that does not mean that people can take up any identity they want, in any way they want, whenever they want; indeed, Edley and Wetherell (1997) suggest that identity construction is constrained by taking account of the circumstances either at hand, or those encountered earlier.

I think that the constraints on identity construction go further than that, however. As I argued in reference to ethnic identity (Galasińska and Galasiński, 2003; Galasiński, 2003), empirical data offers a much more complicated view. The local negotiation of identity is not based merely on locally appropriate discourse, or on our own stories. Provisionality of identity, and its continual negotiation in the local context, is just one dimension of identity construction. The other, operating at the level of the nation, society or social group, provides ready-made templates into which the locally negotiated identity is being placed. It is stability (however dynamic) which provides room for provisionality. These taken-for-granted 'narratives', what it means to be a man, what it means to be a woman, must be re-assessed for the benefit of the local situation. In such a way, I see the local project of identity as being framed not only by intersubjective narratives of gender, but also as provided for by the public discourses available to the social actor.

Let me now examine the issue of how masculine identities might be explored, given this theoretical grounding. It is quite accepted that the fact that biological men or women say something does not make it men's or women's talk. As Schegloff (1997) noted, a speaking woman can also be Californian, Jewish, a mediator, a former weaver and many other things. How do we know that what we are in fact analysing is men's or women's talk? It is a question of relevance of gender: how do we know that when we see a biological man speaking, he speaks *as a man*, that he has taken on masculine identity?

Schegloff (1997) proposes that speakers have to 'orient' themselves towards gender, a list of explicit categories which provide evidence for the analyst that gender is relevant in the interaction. The stance has been found too limiting, both on the grounds of Conversational Analysis (see, e.g., Kitzinger, 2000; Tanaka and Fukushima, 2002) and Critical Discourse Analysis (Wetherell, 1998). If I understand Wetherell's critique correctly, she proposes that certain subject positions cannot but be associated with masculine identities (of certain kind, of course). Even though the interaction participants do not orient themselves to gender or masculinity explicitly, such subject positions as 'on the pull', drunkenness or narratives of engagement in sexual activity construct a certain version of male sexuality and thus masculinity. Wetherell continues by saying that such constructions might have ramifications beyond the control or intention of the social actor. Moreover, such identities are intersubjectively understood and, by relevant response, reinforced in interaction and in the process of inter-action. This interaction, in addition, is also with the discursive resources available to men.

While Wetherell's analyses are convincing, I am not certain how they would work in the context of an interview where the negotiation of identity can be minimal and the analyst does not have the resource of participant take-up. I am particularly uneasy with regard to the notion of constructing contexts which go beyond the control and intention of the participant. In other words, coming back the story of my question about the salt, is it not possible that I could be interpreted as taking on a masculine subject position, especially given the response of my relative? In such a way, we admit that identities, subject positions, can be imposed. In other words, speaking as a parent can be subverted into speaking as a father, not in the process of interaction (that, in fact, is a perfectly possible scenario) but in the process of analysis. My concern is even greater if one takes Stokoe and Smithson's (2001) proposal that the analyst use his or her background knowledge or common sense in the analysis. If identities are locally negotiated, it is not for the analyst to impose certain identity categories upon the participants whose interaction he or she is analysing (see also Coleman, 1990).

However, Wetherell's stance is particularly useful, I think, in that her points are limited to the interaction she analyses. She does not offer a check list of discursive resources which construct gender identity. The stance can be seen as taken up by a number of scholars interested in gender identity, Ochs (1992) being the most succinct when he said that there are few such linguistic resources which index gender, exclusively and directly. This point is taken up by Johnson (1997) and Cameron (1997), who say that the complexity of masculine identities does not allow an assumption that they might be performed in some patterned ways. Cameron (1998a) adds that things are complicated further by the multiplicity of constructs of femininity, and thus, by extension, masculinity. Such constructs, continues Cameron, might in fact be in competition, conflict or contradiction with each other. McIlvenny (2002a), stressing that the theory of performativity of gender lacks empirical grounding, prefers not to ask general questions about how identities are performed. Instead of asking questions such as 'How do lesbians talk?' he prefers to ask questions such as 'How do participants talk such that their lesbianness is made salient and consequential for their activities?' (McIlvenny, 2002a:141).

Recently Swann (2002) asked the question of how the analyst might decide that social actors 'do gender' and provides a comprehensive review of 'warrants' used in research. The options she discusses are quantitative/general patterns, indirect reliance on such patterns, participants' orientation as evidenced in the text, speakers' solicited interpretation, analysts' theoretical positions or intuitions, and speakers' biological sex (Swann, 2002:49). Her answer lies in eclectism, a wide range of methods and warrants for claims about 'doing gender' that might include quantitative approaches. The problem is, however, that

Swann does not put her proposals to test and we do not know how they might actually work in practice.

It seems that the assumption that there are no systematic discursive markers of identity seems to be what one is left with. It is only possible to have insight into the context-bound 'discourse of belonging', one which might change from one situation to another as speakers draw upon different resources, often contradictory, to construct themselves as 'being' or 'belonging' (for narratives with contradictory constructions of identity, see Barker and Galasiński, 2001).

Emotions and masculinity

I would like to come back now to the problem of emotion talk. Does the fact that a man, in a given context, talks about his emotional experience tell us anything about how he performs masculinity? Following from this, can a man speak about his emotional experience and not perform masculinity?

I have little doubt that unless we assume that a man is speaking *as a man*, the language of emotions has nothing to do with the performance of masculine identities. The language of emotions might well construct the actor (Crawford *et al.*, 1992), but from that to assume that it constructs a man (or a woman) is to make all sorts of essentialising assumptions as to the pervasiveness of gender in emotion talk. The language of emotions does not constitute a 'discourse of belonging' or, in the words of West and Fenstermaker (2002:541; see also West and Fenstermaker, 1995), cannot be used to 'do difference', 'creating differences among members of different sex categories'. In that sense talking about emotions has nothing to do with social actors 'doing gender', constructing themselves as gendered subjects. As I argued in Chapter 5, biological men talking about their emotions towards their children were taking subject positions of parents rather than fathers and the emotions did not change that fact. To say that an indirect way of speaking about emotions is a way of constructing masculine identity, finally, is both to make a claim about practices of 'doing masculinity' which I rejected earlier, and to make assumptions as to a systematic discourse marker of identity (an assumption which, following others, I rejected above).

The 'language of emotions' can be part of the 'discourse of belonging', however. Thus, if we assume that a man is speaking *as a man*, and is in one way or another constructing himself as a man, then the language of emotions could in fact help us see how it is done. But note the order in which the analysis is carried out: it is first of all the establishment, by whatever means, that the man is taking up the subject position of a man, and only then can we make decisions as to the language of emotions. In such a way the performance of masculinity, coupled with a strategy of talking about emotions, could in fact shed light as to how the speaker is positioning himself, particularly with regard to others (i.e., how the man positions himself in relationships, particularly emotional relationships).

I would like to flag up here a notion that I suggested with regard to constructions of identities in interaction with written texts (Galasiński, 2003). I argued that literacy resources could be seen as providing social actors with a 'grammar of identity', or relatively fixed discursive resources with which to construct identities. This is indeed how one could see the strategies of emotion talk: as discursive resources at the disposal of men in performing masculinities, which analysts could use as a stepping stone for gaining insight into relationship between the locally performed masculinities and gender ideologies. Finally, we could of course wonder to what extent the talk about emotions is incidental and masculinity is often performed with a distance to others; but this is a matter for further research. Incidentally, discovering that emotions have a special role as a resource for constructing masculinity would in fact be a very interesting find. Such a find would tell us more about the construct of masculinity and the ways it is locally negotiated.

Always a man?

The last question that remains to be answered is whether men can speak about their emotions without being men, without performing masculinity. The answer – in the affirmative – will have become obvious by now. The affirmative answer is predicted both theoretically (talking about emotions is not a way of 'doing gender') and empirically (men talking about emotions do not always take up masculine subject positions): this is the crux of Chapter 5. The similarities in men and women constructing helplessness shown in Chapter 6 also suggest either that the two genders have a similar way of talking about emotions, which it would be quite reasonable to assume, or that the category of 'unemployed' need not be gendered (and I am not saying that it cannot be – it can; I am saying only that it need not). What I would like to propose is that one can suspend gender, that one can become someone whose gender is irrelevant, transparent, non-existent.

I would like to offer another story, a final one, to illustrate the point. Some time ago I was travelling (a very long car journey across Europe) with a friend, a man, a fellow Pole living in the UK. At some point our conversation touched upon our experiences of living abroad. The emotional experience of being immigrants, relationships with our 'far-flung' families, old friends and new friends, formed the core material of the conversation. Now, my contention would be that, at least during that part of the conversation, we suspended our gender: we became simply two Poles living abroad, otherwise the conversation would not have been possible. Not only were we constructing ourselves as such, we were thus constructing each other. And it was within that particular construction that we were able to talk about our families and having children who become bilingual, who speak English with their friends. At that point we became Poles living abroad having children abroad. Was it gendered? No, the interaction was not.

Now, I am not proposing that one could not carry out an analysis similar to that of Cameron (1998b) analysing the 'Is there any ketchup, Vera?' type of question. It may well be that such an analysis would have revealed the presence of gender ideologies in what we said but, at the same time, it presumably would also have shown a host of assumptions about class, age, parenthood and, obviously, nationality. The ideologies, the world view, which are part of any discourse (this is one of the crucial assumptions of CDA) do not necessarily impose identities upon those who use them. My point is significant also in the sense that as much as people would not normally 'read off' Polishness from what I say (even though my accent might indicate that I am from Poland), I am not certain why we should need to assume that gender, or masculinity, could be read off from what I say. People would not automatically read off middle class, whiteness or fatherhood, from what I say. And there is no doubting, I think, that, say, ethnicity, race or class are extremely important in our society. Gender, no doubt again, is a subject position of utmost importance. But is the fact that I am a man more important than the fact that I am Polish? Well, not at the Immigration Service desk at the airport!

Finally, if gender is performative, done in the context, one must assume that the performance may end or change with the fluctuation of the context. It is somewhat akin to situations at academic conferences when people are talking in a shared language but if someone who does not speak that language comes up, they will switch to another language they all understand. The context changes, requiring the participants to accommodate such change. Thus, if the literature assumes that there are multiple versions of masculinity, and that men could perform different versions, why not assume that when a man stops performing one kind of masculinity, instead of beginning to perform another, he does not perform masculinity at all? The moment we assume that the performance can be stopped (and we do by assuming that people can perform different masculinities), it does not follow that it *must* be started. Indeed, call centres, e-mail, examinations or academic book writing all can be genderless, with interactions with call centre staff and through e-mail being situations in which sex categorisation is either difficult or, sometimes, impossible. Note also that I am not saying that they cannot be gendered (they most definitely can) but, importantly, they do not have to be. In this way, in contrast to Weatherall (2002), I think it is for the analyst to establish first *whether* gender is relevant in the interaction before proceeding to demonstrate *how* it is accomplished. It seems to me that it is not only crucial for gender research to establish those contexts which are gendered, but also those which are not, to show the crucial social importance of those that are. And such research would not merely be theoretical; the insight into the mechanisms of genderisation of context, and of subject positions can, in my opinion, be of direct importance to the cause of equality of opportunity for women and men and, in the process, equality of opportunity for people of different racial and ethnic origins, of different ages, abilities, or sexualities.

What about men and emotionality?

Well, men speak about their emotions! In various ways, in various contexts, for different purposes, with different subject positions. But women also speak about their emotions. What is most important is that sometimes they speak about their emotions in exactly the same ways, so perhaps it would be fitting to finish this book about men with two postulates.

First, I would like to second a postulate which has already been made in the literature (e.g., Bing and Bergvall, 1996; Johnson, 1997), which is that the blanket opposition made between men and women is problematic. Also in academe it is part of 'doing difference', exactly of the kind that research into gender analyses. I have no doubt that gender is one of the most crucial axes along which our social life is structured, together with its inequalities, oppressions, discriminations. I am also in no doubt that it is men who are for the most part the oppressors. But saying this is different from arguing that insight into how men speak offers some understanding of masculinity, as contrasted with femininity, 'resulting' from the omnipresence of gender in social life. Academic difference doing seems to me not so different from that the academics more or less critically describe.

The second postulate is about contextualisation of masculinity. It is not about whether men speak about emotions, even though most 'lay' people who asked me what I was writing about said that I would not have to write much since men do not speak about their emotions. This is stereotype overruling common sense, I think. What is considerably more important is that men speak about emotions in particular contexts, in particular ways, occasionally putting their masculinity on one side on becoming fathers, or helpless unemployed. The question is not about multiple masculinities; the question concerns the masculinity or masculinities negotiated here and now. Emotionality in turn, as much as it is part of masculinity as a social construct, is probably not really related to masculine identities. Men speak about their emotions: they do it as men, they do it as parents, they do it as unemployed. But perhaps there are contexts in which masculinity gets entangled with emotionality and becomes part and parcel of the 'discourse of belonging'; this is another path that might be taken up in future

As Commander Riker said of Data:

> Data is a physical representation of a dream, an idea conceived by the mind of a man. His purpose? To serve human needs and interests. He is a collection of neural nets and heuristic algorithms. His responses are dictated by an elaborate software program written by a man. His hardware was built by a man. And a man will turn him off.
>
> (*Star Trek: The Next Generation*: 'The Measure of a Man')

However, we all know that was an oversimplification of that man.

References

Ablon, S., Brown, D., Khantzian, E. J. and Mack, J. E. (eds) (1993) *Human Feelings. Explorations in Affect Development and Meaning*, Hillsdale, NJ: The Analytic Press.

Adams, P., Towns, A. and Gavey, N. (1995) 'Dominance and Entitlement: The Rhetoric Men Use to Discuss their Violence towards Women', *Discourse & Society*, 6 (3): 387–406.

Anderson, K. J. and Leaper, C. (1998) 'Emotion Talk Between Same- and Mixed-Gender Friends. Form and Function', *Journal of Language and Social Psychology*, 17 (4): 419–48.

Apter, T. (1990). *Altered Loves: Mothers and Daughters During Adolescence*, New York: St Martin's.

Apter, T. (1993) 'Altered Views. Fathers' Closeness to Teenage Daughters', in J. Ruthellen and A. Lieblich (eds), *The Narrative Study of Lives*, Vol. 1, Newbury Park/London/New Delhi: Sage: 163–90.

Athanasiadou, A. and Tabakowska, E. (eds) (1998) *Speaking of Emotions. Conceptualisation and Expression*, Berlin/New York: Mouton de Gruyter.

Bamberg, M. (1997a) 'Emotion Talk(s): The Role of Perspective in the Construction of Emotions', in S. Niemeier and R. Dirven (eds), *The Language of Emotions. Conceptualization, Expression, and Theoretical Foundation*, Amsterdam/Philadelphia: John Benjamins: 209–25.

Bamberg, M. (1997b) 'Language, Concepts and Emotions: The Role of Language in Construction of Emotions', *Language Sciences*, 19 (4): 309–40.

Barker, C. (2002) *Making Sense of Cultural Studies*, London/Thousand Oaks/New Delhi: Sage.

Barker, C. and Galasiński, D. (2001) *Cultural Studies and Discourse Analysis. A Dialogue on Language and Identity*, London: Sage.

Barrett, F. (2001) 'The Organizational Construction of Hegemonic Masculinity', in S. M. Whitehead and F. J. Barrett (eds), *The Masculinities Reader*, Cambridge: Polity: 77–99.

Barrett, L. F., Robin, L., Pietromonaco, P. R. and Eyssell, K. M. (1998) 'Are Women the "More Emotional" Sex? Evidence From Emotional Experiences in Social Context', *Cognition and Emotion*, 12 (4): 555–78.

Bavelas, J. Beavin, Black, A., Chovil, N. and Mullett, J. (1990) *Equivocal Communication*, Newbury Park: Sage.

Baxter, J. (2002) 'Competing Discourses in the Classroom: A Post-structuralist Discourse Analysis of Girls' and Boys' Speech in Public Contexts', *Discourse & Society*, 13 (6): 827–42.

Bellelli, G. (1995) 'Knowing and Labelling Emotions', in J. A. Russell, J.-M. Fernández-Dols, A. S. R. Manstead and J. C. Wellenkamp (eds), *Everyday Conceptions of Emotion. An Introduction to the Psychology, Anthropology and Linguistics of Emotion*, Dordrecht/Boston/London: Kluwer Academic Publishers: 491–504.

Bennert, K. and Galasiński, D. (2000) ' "Telling Our Way of Life": Modes of Mediating Social Life in German and Polish Primary-school Textbooks', *Social Semiotics*, 10 (3): 293–312.

Besnier, N. (1995) 'The Appeal and Pitfalls of Cross-disciplinary Dialogues', in J. A. Russell, J.-M. Fernández-Dols, A. S. R. Manstead and J. C. Wellenkamp (eds), *Everyday Conceptions of Emotion. An Introduction to the Psychology, Anthropology and Linguistics of Emotion*, Dordrecht/Boston/London: Kluwer Academic Publishers: 559–70.

Beynon, J. (2002) *Masculinities and Culture*, Buckingham/Philadelphia: Open University Press.

Biddulph, S. (1994) *Manhood*, Sydney: Finch.

Billig, M. (1990a) 'Collective Memory, Ideology and the British Royal Family', in D. Middleton and D. Edwards (eds), *Collective Remembering*, London: Sage: 60–80.

Billig, M. (1990b) 'Stacking the Cards of Ideology: The History of The *Sun Royal Album*', *Discourse & Society*, 1: 17–37.

Billig, M., Condor, S., Edwards, D., Gane, M., Middleton, D. and Radley, A. R. (1988) *Ideological Dilemmas*, London: Sage.

Bing, J. M. and Bergvall, V. L. (1996) 'The Question of Questions: Beyond Binary Thinking', in V. L. Bergvall, J. M. Bing and A. F. Freed (eds), *Rethinking Gender Language and Gender Research*, London: Longman: 1–30.

Blenkenhorn, D. (1995) *Fatherless America*, New York: Basic Books.

Bloch, C. (1996) 'Emotions and Discourse', *Text*, 16 (3): 323–41.

Blommaert, J. (1997) 'Whose Background? Comments on a Discourse-analytic Reconstruction of the Warsaw Uprising', *Pragmatics*, 7: 69–81.

Bodor, P. (1997) 'On the Usage of Emotional Language: A Developmental View of the Tip of an Iceberg', in S. Niemeier and R. Dirven (eds), *The Language of Emotions. Conceptualization, Expression, and Theoretical Foundation*, Amsterdam/Philadelphia: John Benjamins: 195–208.

Böök, M. L. and Penttinen, L. (1997) 'The Portrait of the Unemployed Father in Finnish Women's Magazines', *Journal of Comparative Family Studies*, 28 (3): 262–79.

Bordo, S. (1997) *Twilight Zones*, Berkeley: University of California Press.

Bourdieu, P. (2001) *Masculine Domination*, Oxford: Polity.

Bradac, J., Friedman, E. and Giles, H. (1986) 'A Social Approach to Propositional Communication. Speakers Lie to Hearers', in G. McGregor (ed.), *Language for Hearers*, Oxford: Pergamon Press: 127–51.

Brittan, A. (1989) *Masculinity and Power*, Oxford/New York: Basil Blackwell.

Brody, L. R. (1985) 'Gender Differences in Emotional Development: A Review of Theories and Research', *Journal of Personality*, 53 (2): 102–49.

Brody, L. R. (1993) 'On Understanding Gender Differences in the Expression of Emotion', in S. Ablon, D. Brown, E. J. Khantzian and J. E. Mack (eds), *Human Feelings. Explorations in Affect Development and Meaning*, Hillsdale, NJ: The Analytic Press: 87–121.

Brody, L. R. (1997) 'Gender and Emotion: Beyond Stereotypes', *Journal of Social Issues*, 53 (2): 369–94.

Brody, L. R. (2000) 'The Socialization of Gender Differences in Emotional Expression: Display Rules, Infant Temperament, and Differentiation', in A. H. Fischer (ed.), *Gender and Emotion. Social Psychological Perspectives*, Cambridge: Cambridge University Press: 24–47.

Brown, P. and Levinson, S. (1987) *Politeness*, Cambridge: Cambridge University Press.

Butler, J. (1990) *Gender Trouble*, London: Routledge.

Caffi, C. and Janney, R. W. (1994) 'Toward a Pragmatics of Emotive Communication', *Journal of Pragmatics*, 22: 325–73.

Cameron, D. (1997) 'Performing Gender Identity: Young Men's Talk and the Construction of Heterosexual Masculinity', in S. Johnson and U. H. Meinhof (eds), *Language and Masculinity*, Oxford: Basil Blackwell: 47–64.

Cameron, D. (1998a) 'Gender, Language, and Discourse: A Review Essay', *Signs: Journal of Women in Culture and Society*, 23 (4): 945–73.

Cameron, D. (1998b) ' "Is There Any Ketchup, Vera?": Gender, Power and Pragmatics', *Discourse & Society*, 9 (4): 437–55.

Chapman, R. (1988) 'The Great Pretender: Variations on the New Man Theme', in R. Chapman and J. Rutherford (eds), *Male Order. Unwrapping Masculinity*, London: Lawrence & Wishart: 225–49.

Chouliaraki, L. (1998) 'Regulation in "Progressivist" Pedagogic Discourse: Individualized Teacher–pupil Talk', *Discourse & Society*, 9 (1): 5–32.

Chouliaraki, L. and Fairclough, N. (1999) *Discourse in Late Modernity*, Edinburgh: Edinburgh University Press.

Clare, A. (2001) *On Men. Masculinity in Crisis*, London: Arrow Books.

Clark, M. S. (ed.) (1992) *Emotion and Social Behavior*, Newbury Park: Sage.

Clatterbaugh, K. (1997) *Contemporary Perspectives on Masculinity*, Boulder/Oxford: Westview Press.

Coates, J. (1997) 'One-at-a-time: The Organization of Men's Talk', in S. Johnson and U. H. Meinhof (eds), *Language and Masculinity*, Oxford: Basil Blackwell: 107–29.

Coates, J. (1999) 'Changing Femininities. The Talk of Teenage Girls', in M. Bucholtz, A. C. Liang and L. A. Sutton (eds), *Reinventing Identities. The Gendered Self in Discourse*, New York, Oxford: Oxford University Press: 123–44.

Coates, J. (2003) *Men Talk. Stories in the Making of Masculinities*, Oxford: Basil Blackwell.

Cohen, T. F. (1993) 'What Do Fathers Provide? Reconsidering the Economic and Nurturant Dimensions of Men as Parents', in J. C. Hood (ed.), *Men, Work, and Family*, Newbury Park/London/New Delhi: Sage: 1–22.

Coleman, W. (1990) 'Doing Masculinity/Doing Theory', in J. Hearn and D. Morgan (eds), *Men, Masculinities and Social Theory*, London/Boston/Sydney/Wellington: Unwin Hyman: 186–99.

Coltrane, S. (1997) *Family Man: Fatherhood, Housework, and Gender Family*, New York: Oxford University Press.

Coltrane, S. and Allan, K. (1994) ' "New" Fathers and Old Stereotypes: Representations of Masculinity in 1980s Television Advertising', *Masculinities*, 2 (4): 43–66.

Connell, R. W. (1995) *Masculinities*, Cambridge: Polity.

Connell, R. W. (2000) *The Men and the Boys*, Cambridge: Polity.

Connell, R. W. (2002) *Gender*, Cambridge: Polity.

Crawford, J., Kippax, S., Onyx, J., Gault, U. and Benton, P. (1992) *Emotion and Gender. Constructing Meaning from Memory*, London/Newbury Park/New Delhi: Sage.

Daniels, C. (ed.) (1998) *Lost Fathers*, London: Macmillan.

Dascal, M. (1977) 'Conversational Relevance', *Journal of Pragmatics*, 1: 309–28.

De Beaugrande, R. (1992) 'Topicality and Emotion in the Economy and Agenda of Discourse', *Linguistics*, 30: 243–65.

De Rivera, J. (1992) 'Emotional Climate: Social Structure and Emotional Dynamics', in K. T. Strongman (ed.), *International Review of Studies on Emotion*, Vol. 2, Chichester/New York/Brisbane/Toronto/Singapore: John Wiley: 197–218.

Duncombe, J. and Marsden, D. (1995) ' "Workaholics" and "Whingeing Women": Theorising Intimacy and Emotion Work – the Last Frontier of Gender Inequality?', *Sociological Review*, 43 (1): 150–69.

Duncombe, J. and Marsden, D. (1998) ' "Stepford wives" and "Hollow Men"? Doing Emotion Work, Doing Gender and "Authenticity" in Intimate Heterosexual Relationships', in G. Bendelow and S. J. Williams (eds), *Emotions in Social Life. Critical Themes and Contemporary Issues*, London/New York: Routledge: 211–27.

Edley, N. (2001) 'Analysing Masculinity: Interpretative Repertoires, Ideological Dilemmas and Subject positions', in M. Wetherell, S. Taylor and S. J. Yates (eds), *Discourse as Data*, London: Sage: 189–228.

Edley, N. and Wetherell, M. (1995) *Men in Perspective. Practice, Power and Identity*, Hemel Hempstead: Prentice Hall/Harvester Wheatsheaf.

Edley, N. and Wetherell, M. (1996) 'Masculinity, Power and Identity', in M. Mac an Ghaill (ed.), *Understanding Masculinities*, Buckingham/Philadelphia: Open University Press: 97–113.

Edley, N. and Wetherell, M. (1997) 'Jockeying for Position: The Construction of Masculine Identities', *Discourse & Society*, 8 (2): 203–17.

Edley, N. and Wetherell, M. (1999) 'Imagined Futures: Young Men's Talk about Fatherhood and Domestic Life', *British Journal of Social Psychology*, 38: 181–94.

Edwards, T. (1997) *Men in the Mirror. Men's Fashion, Masculinity and Consumer Society*, London: Cassell.

Ehrlich, S. (2002) 'Legal institutions, nonspeaking recipiency and participants' orientations', *Discourse & Society*, 13 (6): 731–48.

Ekman, P. (1992) 'An Argument for Basic Emotions', *Cognition and Emotion*, 6: 169–200.

Ekman, P. (1993) 'Facial expression and emotion', *American Psychologist*, 48 (4): 384–92.

Ekman, P. and Davidson, R. J. (eds) (1994) *The Nature of Emotion. Fundamental Questions*, New York/Oxford: Oxford University Press.

Enfield, N. J. and Wierzbicka, A. (2002) 'The Body in Description of Emotion', *Pragmatics & Cognition*, 10 (1/2): 1–26.

Fairclough, N. (1989) *Language and Power*, London: Longman.

Fairclough, N. (1992) *Discourse and Social Change*, Oxford: Polity Press.

Fairclough, N. (1995) *Critical Discourse Analysis*, London: Longman.

Fairclough, N. (2003) *Analysing Discourse*, London: Routledge.

Fairclough, N. and Wodak, R. (1997) 'Critical Discourse Analysis', in T. A. van Dijk (ed.), *Discourse as Social Interaction*, London: Sage: 258–84.

Faludi, S. (2000) *Stiffed: The Betrayal of the American Man*, London: Vintage.

Fiehler, R. (2002) 'How to Do Emotions With Words: Emotionality in Conversations', in S. R. Fussell (ed.), *The Verbal Communication of Emotions*, Mahwah: Lawrence Erlbaum Associates: 79–106.

Fischer, A. H. (1993) 'Sex Differences in Emotionality: Fact or Stereotype?', *Feminism & Psychology*, 3 (3): 303–18.

Fischer, A. H. (1995) 'Emotion Concepts as a Function of Gender', in J. A. Russell, J.-M. Fernández-Dols, A. S. R. Manstead and J. C. Wellenkamp (eds), *Everyday Conceptions of Emotion. An Introduction to the Psychology, Anthropology and Linguistics of Emotion*, Dordrecht/Boston/London: Kluwer Academic Publishers: 457–74.

Fischer, A. H. and Jansz, J. (1995) 'Reconciling Emotions with Western Personhood', *Journal for the Theory of Social Behaviour*, 25 (1): 59–80.

Fischer, A. H. and Manstead A. S. R. (2000) 'The Relation Between Gender and Emotion in Different Cultures', in A. H. Fischer (ed.), *Gender and Emotion. Social Psychological Perspectives*, Cambridge: Cambridge University Press: 71–94.

Fivush, R. and Buckner, J. P. (2000) 'Gender, Sadness, and Depression: The Development of Emotional Focus through Gendered Discourse', in A. H. Fischer (ed.), *Gender and Emotion. Social Psychological Perspectives*, Cambridge: Cambridge University Press: 232–53.

Foolen, A. (1997) 'The Expressive Function of Language: Towards a Cognitive Semantic Approach', in S. Niemeier and R. Dirven (eds), *The Language of Emotions. Conceptualization, Expression, and Theoretical Foundation*, Amsterdam/Philadelphia: John Benjamins: 15–32.

Fowler, R. (1985) 'Power', in T. A. Van Dijk (ed.), *Handbook of Discourse Analysis*, Vol. 4, London: Academic Press: 61–82.

Fowler, R. (1991) *Language in the News*, London: Routledge.

Fowler, R. (1996) 'On critical linguistics', in R. C. Caldas-Coulthard and M. Coulthard (eds), *Texts and Practices*, London: Routledge: 3–14.

Fowler, R., Hodge, B., Kress, G. and Trew, T. (eds) (1979) *Language and Control*, London: Routledge.

Gaillie, D., Marsh, C. and Vogler, C. (eds) (1994) *Social Change and the Experience of Unemployment*, Oxford: Oxford University Press.

Galasińska, A. (2003) 'Temporal Shifts in Photo-elicited Narratives in a Polish Border Town', *Narrative Inquiry*, 13 (2): 393–411.

Galasińska, A. and Galasiński, D. (2003) 'Discursive strategies for coping with sensitive topics of the Other', *Journal of Ethnic and Migration Studies*, 29 (5): 849–63.

Galasińska, A., Rollo, C. and Meinhof, U. H. (2002) 'Urban Space and the Construction of Identity on the German-Polish Border', in U. H Meinhof (ed.), *Living (with) Borders. Identity Discourses on East-West Borders in Europe*, Aldershot: Ashgate: 119–39.

Galasiński, D. (1997a) 'The Making of History. Some Remarks on Politicians' Presentation of Historical Events', *Pragmatics*, 7: 55–68.

Galasiński, D. (1997b) 'Background and Discourse Analysis. A Response to Jan Blommaert', *Pragmatics*, 7: 83–8.

Galasiński, D. (2000) *The Language of Deception. A Discourse Analytic Study*, Thousand Oaks: Sage.

Galasiński, D. (2002, June) 'Narratives of Disenfranchised Self in the Polish Post-Communist Reality', Paper presented at the conference on 'Post-Communism: Theory and Practice', University of Warwick, UK.

Galasiński, D. (2003, September) ' "There is Simply no Such Option Here!" Questionnaires and Respondents' Construction of Identity', AILA conference on 'Multiliteracies and Cultural literacy', Ghent, Belgium.

Galasiński, D. and Meinhof, U. H. (2002) 'Looking across the River: German–Polish Border Communities and the Construction of the Other', *Journal of Language and Politics*, 1 (1): 23–58.

Gallois, C. (1993) 'The Language and Communication of Emotion', *American Behavioral Scientist*, 36 (3): 309–38.

Geldof, B. (2003) 'The father love that dare not speak its name', *The Sunday Times*, 7 November.

Giddens, A. (1992) *The Transformation of Intimacy*, Cambridge: Polity Press.

Gilmore, D. D. (1990) *Manhood in the Making*, New Haven: Yale University Press.

Ginsburg, G. P. and Harrington, M. E. (1996) 'Bodily States and Context in Situated Lines of Action', in R. Harré and W. G. Parrott (eds), *The Emotions. Social, Cultural and Biological Dimensions*, London/Thousand Oaks/New Delhi: Sage: 229–58.

Goddard, C. (2002) 'Explicating Emotions Across Languages and Cultures: A Semantic Approach', in S. R. Fussell (ed.), *The Verbal Communication of Emotions*, Mahwah: Lawrence Erlbaum Associates: 19–53.

Goffman, E. (1959) *The Presentation of Self in Everyday Life*, Garden City: Doubleday.

Goleman, D. (1995) *Emotional Intelligence*, London: Bloomsbury.

Goodwin, M. H. (2002) 'Building Power Asymmetries in Girls' Interaction', *Discourse & Society*, 13 (6): 715–30.

Gough, B. and Edwards, G. (1998) 'The Beer Talking: Four Lads, a Carry Out and the Reproduction of Masculinities', *Sociological Review*, 46 (3): 409–35.

Greenwood, J. D. (1994) *Realism, Identity and Emotion*, London/Thousand Oaks/New Delhi: Sage.

Grice, H. P. (1975) 'Logic and Conversation', in P. Cole and J. Morgan (eds), *Speech Acts (Syntax and Semantics 3)*, New York: Academic Press: 41–58.

Hall, S. (1981) 'Encoding/Decoding', in S. Hall *et al.*, *Culture, Media, Language*, London: Hutchinson.

Hall, S. (1996) 'The Problem of Ideology. Marxism without Guarantees', in D. Morley and K. H. Chen (eds), *Stuart Hall Critical Dialogues in Cultural Studies*, London: Routledge: 25–46.

Hall, S. (1997) 'The Work of Representation', in S. Hall (ed.), *Representation: Cultural Representation and Signifying Practices*, London/Thousand Oaks: Sage.

Halliday, M. A. K. (1978) *Language as Social Semiotic*, London: Edward Arnold.

Halliday, M. A. K. (1994) *An Introduction to Functional Grammar* (2nd edition), London: Edward Arnold.

Halliday, M. A. K. and Hasan, R. (1985) *Language, Context, and Text*, Oxford: Oxford University Press.

Hallpike, C. R. (1969) 'Social Hair', *Man*, 4: 256–64.

Harré, R (1991) *Physical Being*, Oxford: Basil Blackwell.

Harré, R. (1986a) 'An Outline of the Social Constructionist Viewpoint', in R. Harré (ed.), *The Social Construction of Emotions*, Oxford: Basil Blackwell: 2–14.

Harré, R. (ed.) (1986b) *The Social Construction of Emotions*, Oxford: Basil Blackwell.

Harré, R. and Parrott, W. G. (eds.) (1996) *The Emotions. Social, Cultural and Biological Dimensions*, London/Thousand Oaks/New Delhi: Sage.

Harré, R. and Stearns, P. (eds) (1995) *Discursive Psychology in Practice*, London/Thousand Oaks/New Delhi: Sage.

Haviland, J. M. and Goldston, R. B. (1992) 'Emotion and Narrative: The Agony and the Ecstasy', in K. T. Strongman (ed.), *International Review of Studies on Emotion*, Vol. 2, Chichester/New York/Brisbane/Toronto/Singapore: John Wiley: 219–48.

Hearn, J. (1993) 'Emotive Subjects: Organizational Men, Organizational Masculinities and the (De)construction of "Emotions" ', in S. Fineman (ed.), *Emotion in Organizations*, London: Sage: 142–66.

Hearn, J. (1996) 'Is Masculinity Dead? A Critique of the Concept of Masculinity/ Masculinities', in M. Mac an Ghaill (ed.), *Understanding Masculinities*, Buckingham/ Philadelphia: Open University Press: 202–17.

Hepworth, M. (1998) 'Ageing and the Emotions', in G. Bendelow and S. J. Williams (eds), *Emotions in Social Life. Critical Themes and Contemporary Issues*, London/ New York: Routledge: 173–89.

Hochschild, A. R. and Machung, A. (1989) *The Second Shift*, Harmondsworth: Penguin Putnam.

Hodge, R. and Kress, G. (1988) *Social Semiotics*, Oxford: Polity Press.

Hodge, R. and Kress, G. (1993) *Language as Ideology*, London: Routledge.

Holdcroft, D. (1987) 'Conversational Relevance', in J. J. Verschueren and M. Bertucelli-Papi (eds), *The Pragmatic Perspective*, Amsterdam: John Benjamins: 477–95.

Hollander, J (2001) 'Doing *Studs*: The Performance of Gender and Sexuality on Late-Night Television', in M. S. Kimmell and M. A. Messner (eds), *Men's Lives*, Boston: Allyn & Bacon: 477–93.

Holmes, J. (1995) *Women, Men and Politeness*, London: Longman.

Honigsbaum, M. (2003) 'Man about the House', *The Observer Magazine*, 30 November.

Hood, J. C. (1986) 'The Provider Role: Its Meaning and Measurement', *Journal of Marriage and the Family*, 48: 349–59.

Hood, J. C. (ed.) (1993) *Men, Work, and Family*, Newbury Park/London/New Delhi: Sage.

Horrocks, R. (1994) *Masculinity in Crisis*, New York: St Martin's.

Howard, C., Tuffin, K. and Stephens, C. (2000) 'Unspeakable Emotion. A Discursive Analysis of Police Talk About Reactions to Trauma', *Journal of Language and Social Psychology*, 19 (3): 295–314.

Jansz, J. (2000) 'Masculine Identity and Restrictive Emotionality', in A. H. Fischer (ed.), *Gender and Emotion. Social Psychological Perspectives*, Cambridge: Cambridge University Press: 166–86.

Jaworski, A. (1993) *The Power of Silence*, London: Sage.

Johnson, J. T. and Shulman, G. A. (1988) 'More Alike than Meets the Eye: Perceived Gender Differences in Subjective Experience and Its Display', *Sex Roles*, 19 (1/2): 67–79.

Johnson, S. (1997) 'Theorizing Language and Masculinity: A Feminist Perspective', in S. Johnson and U. H. Meinhof (eds), *Language and Masculinity*, Oxford: Basil Blackwell: 8–26.

Johnson-Laird, P. N. and Oatley, K. (1989) 'The Language of Emotions: An Analysis of a Semantic Field', *Cognition and Emotion*, 3 (2): 81–123.

Jones, L. (1991) 'Unemployed Fathers and their Children: Implications for Policy and Practice', *Child and Adolescent Social Work Journal*, 8 (2): 101–16.

Kelly, J. R. and Hutson-Comeaux, S. L. (1999) 'Gender-Emotion Stereotypes are Context Specific', *Sex Roles*, 40 (1/2): 107–20.

Kelvin, P. and Jarrett, J. E. (1985) *Unemployment: Its Social Psychological Effects*, Cambridge: Cambridge University Press.

Kemper, T. D. (1991) 'An Introduction to the Sociology of Emotions', in K. T. Strongman (ed.), *International Review of Studies on Emotion*, Vol. 1, Chichester/New York/Brisbane/Toronto/Singapore: John Wiley: 301–49.

Kerfoot, D. (2001) 'The Organization of Intimacy: Mangerialism, Masculinity and Masculine Subject', in S. M. Whitehead and F. J. Barrett, *The Masculinities Reader*, Cambridge: Polity: 233–52.

Kidron, Y. and Kuzar, R. (2002) 'My Face is Paling Against My Will: Emotion and Control in English and Hebrew', *Pragmatics & Cognition*, 10 (1/2): 129–58.

Kiesling, S. F. (1997) 'Power and the Language of Men', in S. Johnson and U. H. Meinhof (eds), *Language and Masculinity*, Oxford: Basil Blackwell: 65–85.

Kimmell, M. S. and Messner, M. A. (eds) (2001) *Men's Lives*, Boston: Allyn & Bacon.

Kitzinger, C. (2000) 'Doing feminist Conversation Analysis', *Feminism and Psychology*, 10 (2): 163–93.

Koczanowicz, L. and Kołodziejska, D. (1999) 'Nation, Identity, Transition', in J. Miklaszewska (ed.), *Democracy in Central Europe 1989–99*, Krakow: Meritum.

Kövecses, Z. (1988) *The Language of Love. Semantics of Passion in Conversational English*, Lewisburg: Bucknell University Press; London and Toronto: Associated University Presses.

Kövecses, Z. (1990) *Emotion Concepts*, New York/Berlin/Heidelberg/London/Paris/Tokyo/Hong Kong: Springer-Verlag.

Kövecses, Z. (1991) 'Happiness: A Definitional Effort', *Metaphor and Symbolic Activity*, 6 (1): 29–46.

Kozłowska, O. (2004) 'Żyć bezrobociem: analiza dyskursu bezrobotnych', MA dissertation, Institute of Psychology, University of Opole, Poland.

Kress, G. and van Leeuwen, T. (1996) *Reading Images*, London: Routledge.

Kulick, D. (2003) 'Review of Coates, J. (2003) *Men Talk. Stories in the Making of Masculinities*, Oxford: Basil Blackwell,' *Journal of Sociolinguistics*, 7 (4): 628–30.

Kuzio, T. (2001) 'Identity and Nation-building in Ukraine: Defining the "Other"', *Ethnicities*, 1 (3): 343–66.

Lakoff, G. (1987) *Women, Fire, and Dangerous Things*, Chicago: University of Chicago Press.

Lakoff, G. and Johnson, M. (1980) *Metaphors We Live By*, Chicago: University of Chicago Press.

Lakoff, R. (1973) 'Language and Woman's Place', *Language in Society*, 2: 45–80.

Lawes, R. (1999) 'Marriage: An Analysis of Discourse', *British Journal of Social Psychology*, 38: 1–20.

Lazar, M. M. (2000) 'Gender, Discourse and Semiotics: The Politics of Parenthood Representations', *Discourse & Society*, 11 (3): 373–400.

Lazarus, R. (1991) *Emotion and Adaptation*, New York: Oxford University Press.

Lazarus, R. (1995) 'Vexing Research Problems Inherent in Cognitive-mediational Theories of Emotion and Some Solutions', *Psychological Inquiry*, 6 (3): 183–96.

Lee, J. (1991) *At My Father's Wedding*, New York: Bantham Books.

Lloyd, M. (1999) 'Performativity, Parody, Politics', *Theory, Culture and Society*, 16 (2): 195–213.

Lupton, D. (1998) *The Emotional Self. Sociocultural Exploration*, London/Thousand Oaks/New Delhi: Sage.

Lupton, D. and Barclay, L. (1997) *Constructing Fatherhood. Discourses and Experiences*, London/Thousand Oaks/New Delhi: Sage.

Lutz, C. A. (1988) *Unnatural Emotions*, Chicago/London: The University of Chicago Press.

Lutz, C. A. (1990) 'Engendered Emotion: Gender, Power, and the Rhetoric of Emotional Control in American Discourse', in C. A. Lutz and L. Abu-Lughod (eds), *Language and the Politics of Emotion*, Cambridge: Cambridge University Press: 69–91.

Lutz, C. A. (1996) 'Engendered Emotion: Gender, Power, and the Rhetoric of Emotional Control in American Discourse', in R. Harré and W. G. Parrott (eds), *The Emotions. Social, Cultural and Biological Dimensions*, London/Thousand Oaks/New Delhi: Sage: 151–70.

Lutz, C. A. and Abu-Lughod, L. (eds) (1990) *Language and the Politics of Emotion*, Cambridge: Cambridge University Press.

Lyndon, N. (1993) *No More Sex*, London: Mandarin.

MacInnes, J. (1998) *The End of Masculinity*, Buckingham/Philadelphia: Open University Press.

Makselon, B. (1998) 'Atrybucje przyczyn utraty pracy a wybór strategii zaradczych przez osoby bezrobotne', in Z. Ratajczak (ed.), *Bezrobocie. Strategie zaradcze i wzorce pomocy psychologiczne*, Katowice: Wydawnictwo Uniwersytetu Śląskiego: 101–9.

Makselon-Kowalska, B. (2001) 'Stereotypy związane z bezrobociem a poczucie własnej tożsamości u osób bezrobotnych', in Z. Ratajczak (ed.), *Bezrobocie: miedzy bezradnością a nadzieja*, Katowice: Wydawnictwo Uniwersytetu Śląskiego: 11–19.

Marody, M. (2000) 'Tożsamość społeczna w okresie przemian', *Czasopismo Psychologiczne*, 6 (3–4): 261–6.

Mattinson, J. (1988) *Work, Love, Marriage: The Impact of Unemployment*, London: Duckworth.

McIlvenny, P. (2002a) 'Critical Reflections on Performativity and the "Un/Doing" of Gender and Sexuality in Talk', in P. McIlvenny (ed.), *Talking Gender and Sexuality*, Amsterdam/Philadelphia: John Benjamins: 111–50.

McIlvenny, P. (2002b) 'Researching Talk, Gender and Sexuality', in P. McIlvenny (ed.), *Talking Gender and Sexuality*, Amsterdam/Philadelphia: John Benjamins: 1–48.

McMahon, A. (1993) 'Male Readings of Feminist Theory: The Psychologisation of Sexual Politics in the Masculinity Literature', *Theory and Society*, 22 (5), 675–96.

Meinhof, U. H. (1997) ' "The most Important Event of My Life!". A Comparison of Male and Female Written Narratives', in S. Johnson and U. H. Meinhof (eds), *Language and Masculinity*, Oxford: Basil Blackwell: 208–28.

Meinhof, U. H. and Galasiński, D (2000) 'Photography, Memory, and the Construction of Identities on the Former East–West German Border', *Discourse Studies*, 2 (3): 323–53.

Melosik, Z. (1996) *Tożsamość, ciało i władza*, Poznań: Wydawnictwo Edytor.

Melosik Z. (2002) *Kryzys męskości w kulturze współczesnej*, Poznań: Wydawnictwo Wolumin.

Menz, F. (1989) 'Manipulation Strategies in Newspapers: A Program for Critical Linguistics', in R. Wodak (ed.), *Language, Power and Ideology*, Amsterdam: John Benjamins: 227–49.

Middleton, P. (1992) *The Inward Gaze. Masculinity and Subjectivity in Modern Culture*, London/New York: Routledge.

Morgan, D. H. J. (1992) *Discovering Men*, London/New York: Routledge.

Morgan, D. H. J. (2001) 'Family, Gender, and Masculinities', in S. M. Whitehead and F. J. Barrett, *The Masculinities Reader*, Cambridge: Polity: 223–32.

Morrison, B. (1993) *And When Did You Last See Your Father?*, London: Granta.

Mulac, A., Bradac, J. J. and Gibbons, P. (2001) 'Empirical Support for the Gender-as-culture Hypothesis', *Human Communication Research*, 27 (1): 121–52.

Nardi, P. M. (ed.) (1992) *Men's Friendships*, Newbury Park/London/New Delhi: Sage.

Nonn, T. (2001) 'Hitting Bottom: Homelessness, Poverty, and Masculnity', in M. S. Kimmell and M. A. Messner (eds), *Men's Lives*, Boston: Allyn & Bacon: 242–51.

Oatley, K. and Jenkins, J. M. (1996) *Understanding Emotions*, Cambridge, MA: Basil Blackwell.

Ochs, E. (1992) 'Indexing Gender', in A.Duranti and C.Goodwin (eds), *Rethinking Context*, Cambridge: Cambridge University Press: 335–58.

Ochs, E. and Schieffelin, B. (1989) 'Language Has a Heart', *Text*, 9 (1): 7–25.

Ochs, E. and Taylor, C. (1995) 'The "Father Knows Best" Dynamic in Dinnertime Narratives', in K. Hall and M. Bucholtz (eds), *Gender Articulate*, New York: Routledge: 100–17.

Parrott, W. G. (1995) 'The Heart and the Head', in J. A. Russell, J.-M. Fernández-Dols, A. S. R. Manstead and J. C. Wellenkamp (eds), *Everyday Conceptions of Emotion. An Introduction to the Psychology, Anthropology and Linguistics of Emotion*, Dordrecht/Boston/London: Kluwer Academic Publishers: 73–84.

Pavlenko, A. (2002a) 'Bilingualism and Emotions', *Multilingua*, 21(1): 45–78.

Pavlenko, A. (2002b) 'Emotions and the Body in Russian and English', *Pragmatics & Cognition*, 10 (1/2): 207–42.

Pecheux, M. (1982) *Language Semantics and Ideology*, London: Macmillan.

Planalp, S. (1999) *Communicating Emotion. Social, Moral, and Cultural Processes*, Cambridge: Cambridge University Press.

Pleck, J. (1987) 'American Fathering in Historical Perspective', in M. Kimmel (ed.), *Changing Men: New Directions in Research on Men and Masculinity*, Beverly Hills: Sage: 83–97.

Pleck, J. H., Sonenstein, F. L. and Ku, L. C. (1993) 'Masculinity Ideology: Its Impact on Adolescent Males' Heterosexual Relationships', *Journal of Social Issues*, 49 (3): 11–29.

Pujolar, J. (2000) *Gender, Heteroglossia and Power*, Berlin: Mouton de Gruyter.

Pyke, K. D. (1996) 'Class-Based Masculinities. The Interdependence of Gender, Class, and Interpersonal Power', *Gender & Society*, 10 (5): 527–79.

Reid, H. M. and Fine, G. A. (1992) 'Self-Disclosure in Men's Friendships: Variations Associated with Intimate Relations', in P. M. Nardi (ed.), *Men's Friendships*, Newbury Park/London/New Delhi: Sage: 132–52.

Rosenberg, D. V. (1990) 'Language in the Discourse of the Emotions', in C. A. Lutz and L. Abu-Lughod (eds), *Language and the Politics of Emotion*, Cambridge: Cambridge University Press: 162–85.

Rutherford, J. (1988) 'Who's That Man?', in R. Chapman and J. Rutherford (eds), *Male Order. Unwrapping Masculinity*, London: Lawrence & Wishart: 21–67.

Rutherford, J. (1992) *Men's Silences. Predicaments in Masculinity*, London/New York: Routledge.

Ryba, M. (2003) 'Narracje mężczyzn zarabiających mniej od swoich żon', MA dissertation, Institute of Psychology, University of Opole, Poland.

Saarni, C. (1999) *The Development of Emotional Competence*, New York: Guilford.

Sanders, R. E. (1987) *Cognitive Foundations of Calculated Speech*, New York: State University of New York Press.

Sarangi, S. K. and Slembrouck, S. (1992) 'Non-cooperation in Communication: A Reassessment of Gricean Pragmatics', *Journal of Pragmatics*, 17: 117–54.

Schegloff, E. (1997) 'Whose text? Whose context?', *Discourse & Society*, 8 (2): 165–87.

Seidler, V. J. (1988) 'Fathering, Authority and Masculinity', in R. Chapman and J. Rutherford (eds), *Male Order. Unwrapping Masculinity*, London: Lawrence & Wishart: 272–302.

Seidler, V. J. (1989) *Rediscovering Masculinity*, London: New York.

Seidler, V. J. (1992) 'Rejection, Vulnerability, and Friendship', in P. M. Nardi (ed.), *Men's Friendships*, Newbury Park/London/New Delhi: Sage: 15–34.

Seidler, V. J. (1994) *Unreasonable Men*, London: Routledge.

Shields, S. A. (1987) 'Women, Men, and the Dilemma of Emotion', in P. Shaver and C. Hendrick (eds), *Sex and Gender*, Newbury Park/Beverly Hills/London/New Delhi: Sage: 229–50.

Shields, S. A. (1990) 'Conceptualising the Biology-Culture Relationship in Emotion: An Analogy with Gender', *Cognition and Emotion*, 4 (4): 359–74.

Shields, S. A. (1991) 'Gender in the Psychology of Emotion: A Selective Research Review', in K. T. Strongman (ed.), *International Review of Studies on Emotion*, Vol. 1, Chichester/New York/Brisbane/Toronto/Singapore: John Wiley: 227–46.

Shields, S. A. (1995) 'The Role of Emotion Beliefs and Values in Gender Development', in N. Eisenberg (ed.), *Social Development*, Thousand Oaks/London/New Delhi: Sage: 212–32.

Shields, S. A. (2000) 'Thinking about Gender, Thinking about Theory: Gender and Emotional Experience', in A. H. Fischer (ed.), *Gender and Emotion. Social Psychological Perspectives*, Cambridge: Cambridge University Press: 3–23.

Shields, S. A. (2002) *Speaking from the Heart. Gender and the Social Meaning of Emotion*, Cambridge: Cambridge University Press.

Shields, S. A. and Crowley, J. J. (1996) 'Appropriating Questionnaires and Rating Scales for a Feminist Psychology: A Multi-method Approach to Gender and Emotion', in S. Wilkinson (ed.), *Feminist Social Psychologies*, Buckingham: Open University Press: 218–232.

Shields, S. A. and MacDowell, K. A. (1987) ' "Appropriate" Emotion in Politics: Judgments of a Televised Debate', *Journal of Communication*, 37: 78–89.

Shimanoff, S. B. (1985) 'Expressing Emotions in Words: Verbal Patterns of Interaction', *Journal of Communication*, 35: 16–31.

Stacey, J. (1996) *In the Name of the Family; Rethinking Family Values in a Postmodern World*, Boston: Beacon Press.

Stearns, P. (1995) 'Emotion', in R. Harré and P. Stearns (eds), *Discursive Psychology in Practice*, London/Thousand Oaks/New Delhi: Sage: 37–54.

Stearns, P. N. (1979) *Be a Man! Males in Modern Society*, New York/London: Holmes & Meier.

Stokoe, E. H. and Smithson, J. (2001) 'Making Gender Relevant: Conversations Analyst and Gender Categories in Interaction', *Discourse & Society*, 12 (2): 217–44.

Strongman, K. T. (1996) *The Psychology of Emotion*, New York: John Wiley.

Su, S. P. (1994) *Lexical Ambiguity in Poetry*, London: Longman.

Sullivan, O. (2000) 'The Division of Domestic Labour: Twenty Years of Change?', *Sociology*, 34 (3): 437–56.

Sunderland, J. (2002) 'Baby Entertainer, Bumbling Assistant and Line Manager. Discourse of Paternal Identity in Parentcraft Texts', in L. Litosseliti and J. Sunderland (eds), *Gender Identity and Discourse Analysis*, Amsterdam/Philadelphia: John Benjamins: 293–324.

Sunderland, J. and Litosseliti, L. (2002) 'Gender Identity and Discourse Analysis. Theoretical and Empirical Considerations', in L. Litosseliti and J. Sunderland (eds), *Gender Identity and Discourse Analysis*, Amsterdam/Philadelphia: John Benjamins: 3–39.

Swain, S. O. (1992) 'Men's Friendships with Women: Intimacy, Sexual Boundaries, and the Informant Role', in P. M. Nardi (ed.), *Men's Friendships*, Newbury Park/London/New Delhi: Sage: 153–71.

Swann, J. (2002) 'Yes, but is it gender?', in L. Litosseliti and J. Sunderland (eds), *Gender Identity and Discourse Analysis*, Amsterdam/Philadelphia: John Benjamins: 43–67.

Synnott, A. (1993) *The Body Social*, London: Routledge.

Talbot, M., Atkinson, K. and Atkinson, D. (2003) *Language and Power in the Modern World*, Edinburgh: Edinburgh University Press.

Tanaka, H. and Fukushima, M. (2002) 'Gender Orientations to Outward Appearance in Japanese Conversation: A Study in Grammar and Interaction', *Discourse & Society*, 13 (6): 749–66.

Tannen, D. (1998) 'Talk in the Intimate Relationships', in J. Coates (ed.), *Language and Gender*, Oxford: Blackwell: 435–45.

Tannen, D. (1999) 'The Display of (Gendered) Identities in Talk at Work', in M. Bucholtz, A. C. Liang and L. A. Sutton (eds), *Reinventing Identities. The Gendered Self in Discourse*, New York/Oxford: Oxford University Press: 221–40.

Thomas, J. (1995) *Meaning in Interaction*, London: Longman.

Thomas, J. L. (1994) 'Older Men as Fathers and Grandfathers', in E. H. Thompson (ed.), *Older Men's Lives*, Thousand Oaks/London/New Delhi: Sage: 197–217.

Thompson, E. H., Pleck, J. H. and Ferrera, D. L. (1992) 'Men and Masculinities: Scales for Masculinity Ideology and Masculinity-Related Constructs', *Sex Roles*, 27 (11/12): 573–607.

Tolson, A. (1977) *The Limits of Masculinity*, London: Tavistock.

Van Dijk, T. A. (1993) 'Principles of Critical Discourse Analysis', *Discourse & Society*, 4: 249–83.

Van Dijk, T. A. (1997) 'The Study of Discourse', in T. A. van Dijk (ed.), *Discourse as Structure and Process*, London: Sage: 1–34.

Van Dijk, T. A. (1998) *Ideology*, London: Sage.

Van Langenhove, L. and Harré, R. (1993) 'Positioning and Autobiography: Telling Your Life', in N. Coupland and J. F. Nussbaum (eds), *Discourse and Lifespan Identity*, Newbury Park: Sage: 81–99.

Van Leeuwen, T. and Wodak, R. (1999) 'Legitimising Immigration: A Discourse-historical Approach', *Discourse Studies*, 1: (1): 83–118.

Verschueren, J. (1999) 'Whose Discipline? Some Critical Reflections on Linguistic Pragmatics', *Journal of Pragmatics*, 31: 89–879.

Walker, K. (1994) ' "I'm not Friends the Way She's Friends": Ideological and Behavioral Constructions of Masculinity in Men's Friendships', *Masculinities*, 2 (2): 38–55.

Weatherall, A. (2002) 'Towards Understanding Gender and Talk-in-interaction', *Discourse & Society*, 13 (6): 767–82.

West, C. and Fenstermaker, S. (1995) 'Doing Difference', *Gender & Society*, 9 (8): 8–37.

West, C. and Fenstermaker, S. (2002) 'Accountability in Action: The Accomplishment of Gender, Race and Class in a Meeting of the University of California Board of Regents', *Discourse & Society*, 13 (4): 537–63.

West, C. and Zimmerman, D. H. (1987) 'Doing Gender', *Gender & Society*, 1 (2): 125–51.

Wetherell, M. (1996) 'Romantic Discourse and Feminist Analysis: Interrogating Investment, Power and Desire', in S. Wilkinson and C. Kitzinger (eds), *Feminism and Discourse*, London: Sage: 128–44.

Wetherell, M. (1998) 'Positioning and Interpretative Repertoires: Conversation Analysis and Post-Structuralism in Dialogue', *Discourse & Society*, 9 (3): 387–412.

Whitehead, S. M. (2002) *Men and Masculinities*, Cambridge: Polity.

Whitehead, S. M. and Barrett, F. J. (2001) 'The Sociology of Masculinity', in S. M. Whitehead and F. J. Barrett, *The Masculinities Reader*, Cambridge: Polity: 1–26.

Wierzbicka, A. (1988) 'The Semantics of Emotions: *Fear* and its Relatives in English', *Australian Journal of Linguistics*, 10: 359–75.

Wierzbicka, A. (1994) 'Emotion, language, and cultural scripts', in S. Kitayama and H. R. Markus (eds), *Emotion and Culture*, Washington, DC: American Psychological Association: 133–96.

Wierzbicka, A. (1995) 'Everyday Conceptions of Emotion: A Semantic Perspective', in J. A. Russell, J.-M. Fernández-Dols, A. S. R. Manstead and J. C. Wellenkamp (eds), *Everyday Conceptions of Emotion. An Introduction to the Psychology, Anthropology and Linguistics of Emotion*, Dordrecht/Boston/London: Kluwer Academic Publishers: 17–47.

Wierzbicka, A. (1998) ' "Sadness" and "Anger" in Russian: The Non-universality of the So-called "Basic Human Emotions" ', in A. Athanasiadou and E. Tabakowska (eds), *Speaking of Emotions. Conceptualisation and Expression*, Berlin/New York: Mouton de Gruyter: 3–28.

Wierzbicka, A. (1999) *Emotions Across Languages and Cultures: Diversity and Universals*, Cambridge: Cambridge University Press.

Wilkinson, S. (1996) 'Feminist Social Psychologies: A Decade of Development', in S. Wilkinson (ed.), *Feminist Social Psychologies. International Perspectives*, Buckingham/Philadelphia: Open University Press: 1–18.

Williams, S. J. (2001) *Emotion and Social Theory. Corporeal Reflections on the (Ir)Rational*, London/Thousand Oaks/New Delhi: Sage.

Willis, P. (2000) *Ethnographic Imagination*, Cambridge: Polity.

Willott, S. and Griffin, C. (1996) 'Men, Masculinity and the Challenge of Long-term Unemployment', in M. Mac an Ghaill (ed.), *Understanding Masculinities*, Buckingham/Philadelphia: Open University Press: 77–92.

Willott, S. and Griffin, C. (1997) ' "Wham Bam, am I a Man?": Unemployed Men Talk about Masculinities', *Feminism & Psychology*, 7 (1): 107–28.

Wodak, R. (1999) 'Critical Discourse Analysis at the End of the 20th Century', *Research on Language and Social Interaction*, 32: 185–93.

Zeldin, T. (1998) *An Intimate History of Humanity*, London: Vintage.

Index

CPSIA information can be obtained at www.ICGtesting.com
Printed in the USA
LVOW120832140513

333704LV00013B/254/P